THE STOIC COMEDIANS

with drawings by
Guy Davenport

THE STOIC COMEDIANS

Flaubert, Joyce, and Beckett

by Hugh Kenner

University of California Press
Berkeley, Los Angeles, London

University of California Press
Berkeley and Los Angeles, California

University of California Press, Ltd.
London, England

California Paperback Edition 1974
ISBN: 0-520-02584-9
Library of Congress Catalog Card Number: 73-85791

Printed in the United States of America

This book is for Walter J. Ong, S.J.

Author's Note

THE SUBSTANCE of this book was presented in the form of three lectures at the Third Annual Georgetown University Conference on Contemporary Literary Criticism, July 1961. Chapter 1 has been published in *Spectrum* (Fall-Winter, 1961). I have since incorporated into chapter 2 much of a paper called "The Book as Book," which was delivered as a Moody Lecture at the University of Chicago in November 1960, and later published in *Christianity and Culture,* edited by J. Stanley Murphy, C.S.B. (Helicon Press, Baltimore, 1961). Chapter 3 has been reshaped in the light of yet another paper, "Art in a Closed Field," which was read at Haverford College (the Shipley Lecture, 1962) and at the University of Virginia (the Peters Rushton Seminars, March 1962), and published in the *Virginia Quarterly Review* (Autumn 1962). I am indebted to the sponsoring bodies and editors concerned for incentive to compose and permission to reprint.

The illustrations are intended to keep the reader from dwelling on the paucity of documentation.

Contents

Illustrations

Damn the nature of things!

RICHARD PORSON (1759-1808)

Preface

THE STOIC is one who considers, with neither panic nor indifference, that the field of possibilities available to him is large perhaps, or small perhaps, but closed. Whether because of the invariable habits of the gods, the invariable properties of matter, or the invariable limits within which logic and mathematics deploy their forms, he can hope for nothing that adequate method could not foresee. He need not despair, but the most fortunate resolution of any predicament will draw its elements still from a known set, and so will ideally occasion him no surprise. The analogies that underlie his thinking are physical, not biological: things are chosen, shuffled, combined; all motion rearranges a limited supply of energy. He has been typically, at typical points in history, an ethical theorist weighing duty against preference without extravagant expectations, a hero aware that in defying the gods he yet fulfills their will, a gambler calculating odds, a proponent of the Second Law of Thermodynamics, and in our time a novelist filling four hundred empty pages with combinations of twenty-six different letters.

It has taken us several centuries to realize how the Gutenberg Revolution transformed literary composition into a potentially Stoical act. So long as writing was the graph of speech, its highly stylized limitations, its nuances synthesized from discrete particles, were tacitly allowed for. Tones, gestures, live inflections, meeting eyes, these catalysts for the continuum of dialogue the reader learns unconsciously to supply. Not only was reading for many centuries an operation always performed with the voice, not merely the eye, but writing, even writing for the press, was controlled by the presupposition that these words here chosen would ideally be animated by speech. "Verie devout asses they were. . . ."—five words of Nashe's, and we know that we hear a voice. But by 1926, I. A. Richards found it necessary to labor the point that *tone* ("the attitude of the speaker to the audience") was one of the components of meaning, for the meaning of printed words had by that time come apart into components which the skilled reader has learned to put back together; and by mid-century a chief occupation of the college classroom had become the effort to persuade eighteen-year-olds, skilled consumers of print for two-thirds of their lives, that there were any kinds of meaning latent in language except the ones a grammar and dictionary will lock together.

> I wonder, by my troth, what thou, and I
> Did, till we lov'd? were we not wean'd till then?

A student who finds those lines clotted has no difficulty with the following:

> On newstands, the new Sunday paper had a clean, uncluttered look (six columns to the page instead of the customary eight), and it was certainly easy to carry home (8 oz. *v.* the 4 lb. 2 oz. of *The New York Times*).

Yet the latter passage is virtually impossible to read aloud. It has moved from research through typewriter to printing press without the intervention of the human voice. I copied it, of course, from the issue of *Time* that happened to be lying nearest me: the entire issue, ninety-two pages of it, a dense mosaic of factuality behind each atom of which is alleged to stand a researcher's guarantee that justification can be produced on demand. *Time,* the exhalation of the linotype machine, does not talk, it compresses. Its very neologisms (cinemactor, Americandidly) carry their wit to the eye alone. In its immense success we behold several million readers a week absorbing information from the printed page by solely visual means, deciphering with ease and speed a mode of language over which, for the first time on so vast a scale, speech has no control at all.

This means that we have grown accustomed at last not only to silent reading, but to reading matter that itself implies nothing but silence. We are skilled in a wholly typographic culture, and this is perhaps the distinguishing skill of twentieth-century man. The language of printed words has become, like the language of mathematics, voiceless; so much so that to meet the demands of writing that does imply the movements of a voice is itself a skill, highly specialized and grown increasingly rare. And simultaneously we have begun to encounter much theory concerning language as a closed field. To program a translating machine, for example, you must treat each of two languages as (1) a set of elements and (2) a set of rules for dealing with those elements. These rules, correctly stated, will generate all possible sentences of the language to which they apply, and of this concept the sentences in a given book may be regarded as special cases. It will be objected that this is a strange way to talk about the Gospel according to St. John. It is; and when we talk of a body of specifiable mass describing an elliptical path at one focus of which spins a globe of ionized atoms, that is an equally strange way to be talking of the earth on which we walk.

That earth was invented in the seventeenth century, when so much else was invented. Invention moved on. By 1780 the mind of Europe had excogitated the Dark Ages, the middle classes, the mercantile spirit, Virtue clothed in Roman togas, enlightened Frenchmen, humorous Englishmen, the past as object of knowledge, the future as arena of betterment, polite society, universal Reason, improving books, useful knowledge, facts and the duty of collecting them, opinion and the need to guide it, sobriety the leveler of all things, and Posterity our concern for whose interests justifies (does it not?) so much unstillness. The same men who called all this bric-à-brac into existence also fussed with Universal Languages; these were an early project of the Royal Society, and for a time detained the great Newton. Printers stunned spelling into conformity, lexicographers language, and encyclopaedists opinion, so that Posterity could enjoy the convenience of forming its words, its sentiments or its notions out of interchangeable parts. And there came into being likewise a class of men whose business it was to set ideas, or sentences or letters, into one likely order or another, to the end that the printing presses might be kept busy and Posterity enlightened; and so numerous were the likely patterns into which words, or sentences, or sentiments could be ordered that these men were very busy indeed. Lemuel Gulliver reported helpfully on how the craft was managed in Lagado, with a machine which shook the entire vocabulary into chance arrangements; and wherever thirty-six scrutineers "found three or four words together that might make part of a sentence, they dictated to the four remaining boys who were scribes."

Amid all this dust there took form the species of literary composition we call the Novel. This is a long work in prose which from the first has fulfilled two requirements:

(1) *Verisimilitude.* This means that the book shall abound in words which name objects familiar to its reader, and in sentences describing pieces of behavior or imitating pieces of conversation which the reader finds recognizable.

(2) *Plausibility.* This means that the progression of events which the work purports to chronicle shall at every point satisfy criteria of reason, since it is the reader's belief that his own actions are reasonable, and he will employ his book-reading time on nothing less. ("Being advised to alter my condition," writes the excellent L. Gulliver, "I married Mrs. Mary Burton, second daughter to Mr. Edmund Burton, hosier in Newgate-street, with whom I received four hundred pounds for a portion.")

The form so circumscribed has this peculiarity, that it tempts subverters; and the significant history of fiction is defined by a list of practitioners who found in its curious rules a challenge. Jane Austen, for instance, is scrupulous, page by page, in consulting the demands of Verisimilitude and Plausibility, but in her presence the readers whose Truth and whose Reason are most directly mirrored feel just a little faint, a little chilly, a little inclined to wonder if the presiding spirit is wholly sympathetic.

But Jane Austen worked with eggshell caution. It was 1850 before the art beloved of the middle classes had been turned with hearty compliance into exactly what it is, a parody of itself, and adapted, furthermore, to just those ultimate criteria of truth, the scientific, which the middle classes most delight to honor; and the middle classes were so disturbed on being given what they had always clamored for that they ordered *Madame Bovary* placed on trial as a massive affront to morals and religion. Flaubert is the first of the Stoic Comedians, obeying scrupulously the rules of the game which he came to see implied the entire Enlightenment, in whose course the game itself had been devised. And the Enlightenment having invented the modern world, Flaubert was driven at last to fiction of encyclopaedic scope; nor even here does one evade the Enlightenment, which invented the Encyclopaedia.

It is evident to the Stoic Comedian that the writer's work is to write. He writes, however, under some disadvantage, for others are so much more fluent than he. It normally takes him upwards of five years to compose a book. What are Joyce's gifts for the manufacture of fiction, beside those of Jack London? Write, though, he does: and it is difficult work, entailing dictionaries, lists, research, bales of documents (one might think he was engaged at something serious), spiritual agonies (and no wonder, since the fiction writer's job is telling lies). If he has not the gift for spinning fiction he can mime the possessors of that gift. ("The summer evening had begun to fold the world in its mysterious embrace": Joyce achieved that sentence one morning, and no doubt promptly sacrificed an ox to Marie Corelli.) And he can, thanks to his detachment from the heat of creation, at least set periods and commas exactly right, depart from sound grammar only knowingly, and be at pains to verify the quantities of useful information for which we look to fiction ("Constipation is a sign of health in pomeranians," Beckett informs us, he who is so chary of risking information.) He could not, we know, improvise a tale by the fireside, not to save his life; but he is enough the master of Gutenberg technology to fabricate the traces of a tale out of printed signs. And it is here, as skilled consumers of print, that we find our usual world intersecting his. We have been working our way for centuries through a world fragmented into typographical elements, and lo, the Comedian has gone before us.

Flaubert and his major successors, Joyce and Beckett, each scorching in turn the earth where his successor would sow his crop, carried forward the novel as Knowing Machine, lifelike, logical, for a hundred years. If during that time there has flourished a different fictional tradition altogether, the tradition of Dostoevski, Tolstoi, George Eliot, D. H. Lawrence, for which the unit is not the sentence but the event, the person not a product but an energy, and the vision not a satire but perhaps an apocalypse,[1] it has flourished thanks in part to the success of the Stoic Comedians in keeping the machine-novel busily at bay; and it flourishes, incidentally, at some risk, the risk of one day losing its spell and seeming less packed with wisdom than with illusion, less pregnant with compassion than cankered with the sentimentalities of a time that supposed the unaided storyteller capable of commanding heavens to open. Flaubert, Joyce and Beckett are their own greatest inventions, and the books they contrived, or had their contrivances contrive, record a century of intellectual history with intricate and moving fidelity: suffering our partner the machine to mechanize all that the hand can do yet remaining obstinately, gaily, living; courting a dead end but discovering how not to die.

[1] See Marvin Mudrick, "Character and Event in Fiction," *Yale Review,* Winter 1961.

1. Gustave Flaubert:

COMEDIAN OF THE ENLIGHTENMENT

I

THE ENLIGHTENMENT lingers in our intellectual histories as a puzzling phenomenon, puzzling because it is so hard to say briefly what it was. It lacks chronology, it lacks locality, it lacks identity. It is personified by no convenient heroes, being by definition antiheroic. Diderot and D'Alembert are rather examples than exemplars. It perhaps hardly knew that it was happening, or not much more than the Middle Ages knew that they were happening, and we may perhaps speculate that the Romantic Movement was the first such event that did know that it was happening, and that this was where the romanticism lay. The Enlightenment seems in retrospect a sort of mystical experience through which the mind of Europe passed, and by which the memory of Europe remains haunted. We carry with us still one piece of baggage from those far-off days, and that is the book which nobody wrote and nobody is expected to read, and which is marketed as The Encyclopaedia: Britannica, Americana, Antarctica or other.

The Encyclopaedia, like its cousin the Dictionary, takes all that we know apart into little pieces, and then arranges

GUSTAVE FLAUBERT: *Comedian of the Enlightenment*

those pieces so that they can be found one at a time. It is produced by a feat of organizing, not a feat of understanding. No Bacon, no Aquinas, is tracing the hierarchies of a human knowledge which he has assumed the responsibility of grasping. If the Encyclopaedia means anything as a whole, no one connected with the enterprise can be assumed to know what that meaning is. A hundred contributors, or a thousand, each responsible for squinting at creation through a single knothole, can work in utter isolation, very likely in a hundred different cities, each on his self-contained packet of knowledge; and these packets an editor with a flow-chart may coordinate, if at all, by appending cross-references, and organize only by filing each in its alphabetical place. That the great *Encyclopédie* contained cross-references to articles which did not exist is not surprising under the circumstances, nor is the presence of wholesale contradiction within the covers of any such bound set; nor, finally, the nearly surrealist discontinuity of the final product. The compendia of which Pliny's *Natural History* is the first extant example have a discursive plan, and later compilations have a hierarchic plan, like the Arts Curriculum. Thus Bartholomew de Glanville, an English Franciscan friar, wrote about 1360 a most popular work, *De proprietatibus rerum*, in 19 books, beginning with God and the angels and ending with colors, scents, flavors and liquors, with a list of 36 eggs; and in the next century "A very popular small encyclopaedia, *Margarita philosophica* (1496), in 12 books, was written by Georg Reisch, a German, prior of the Carthusians of Freiburg, and confessor of the emperor Maximilian I. Books 1-7 treat of the seven liberal arts; 8, 9, principles and origin of natural things; 10, 11, the soul, vegetative, sensitive and intellectual; 12, moral philosophy." (I am quoting from the *Encyclopaedia Britannica* article on Encyclopaedias.) But open the *Encyclopaedia Britannica* itself, and the first topic on which you will receive instruction is the letter A, and the second is the meaning of the term "A-1 at Lloyd's," and the fourteenth is the Aardvark. This is sublimely nonsensical, like conversation in Wonderland, and when G. K. Chesterton remarked at the opening of this century that Nonsense was the literature of the future, we may be sure that he had not only the "Alice" books in the back of his mind but the Britannica, 9th edition, at his elbow. (Chesterton later wrote the article on Humor for the 11th edition. I find it curious that there is no article on Nonsense.)

The mark of the Encyclopaedia, then, is its fragmentation of all that we know into little pieces so arranged that they can be found one at a time. Nothing, except when a cross-reference is provided, connects with or entails anything else; nothing corrects anything else, or affords perspective on anything else. And nobody, consequently, is talking to anyone else. Least of all is the contributor talking to the reader, for there is no way in which the contributor can form the least idea who the reader is. The only entrance requirement is that he be able to use the alphabet; beyond that, his credentials are anybody's guess. Is he the master of his subject, looking for a handy digest of one portion of it? The author of the article on Quaternions prefers to think so. Is his general knowledge extensive, except for the particulars of the subject under discussion? So supposes the expert on the Renaissance. Is he, however, perhaps the veriest tyro, stuffed with just such general notions as will enable him to read a column of moderately undemanding prose, with constant exclamations of astonishment? That is what the authority on Waterfalls has clearly decided. Above all, is he going to relate one subject to another? It is devoutly to be hoped that he is not; for were any diligent soul to attempt a correlation between "Eliot, T. S.," "English Literature—Twentieth Century," and "Poetry, American," all concerned might find themselves saddled with some exceedingly awkward correspondence. Or perhaps not; there is always the hope that the reader will exhibit Pécuchet's syndrome, and give it up.

II

Pécuchet and his friend Bouvard invariably do give it up, but they never lack energy for a new beginning. Flaubert himself gave up, after thirteen months of inventing and chronicling their researches, but in two years he resumed this most exacting of labors, with a ferocity that did not again flag until his death. The truncated *Bouvard et Pécuchet* survives, a Pyrrhic victory over Gutenberg's empire. "As for Molière's comedies," declaimed Augustine Scribe before the Académie Française, "what have they to tell us of the great events of the age of Louis XIV? Have they a word to say about the errors, the weaknesses, the failings of the king? Do they so much as mention the revocation of the Edict of Nantes? . . ." And taking in his hand the printed transcript of this oration, Flaubert wrote in the margin:

"Revocation of the Edict of Nantes: 1685.
"Death of Molière: 1673."

He conceived Bouvard and Pécuchet as two men who should enact, in all innocence, on a heroic scale, just such a reduction to zero of universal, of encyclopaedic, nullity.

And with what Odyssean zest do they read, mark and regurgitate, burning through libraries like a prairie fire! They are the Questing Heroes of an age that is still ours; a Duplex Hercules assaulting jungles, clearing swamps; a bipartite

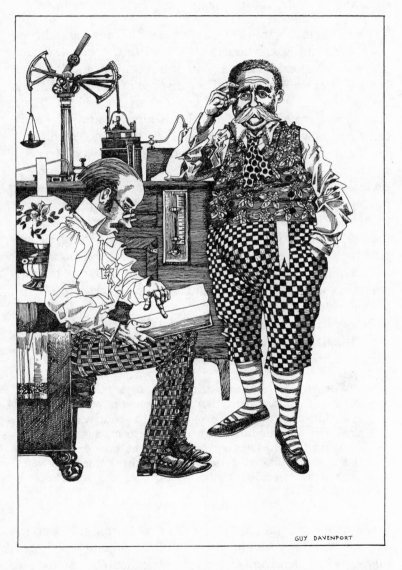

Fig. 1 Pécuchet reading to Bouvard

GUSTAVE FLAUBERT: *Comedian of the Enlightenment*

Theseus venturing into the Labyrinth with transit and theodolite. Chimera after chimera they confront, exhaust, drain, discard. Seven dragons are slain of a morning, and the land is bare after their passing. They dispose of Ancient History in 300 words; it is obscure from lack of documents. They turn to modern history, where the documents are so numerous they grow confused "through their ignorance of dates." Undaunted, they engorge a mnemonic system which has the advantage of combining three other systems; thus "Fenaigle divides the universe into houses, which contain rooms, each having four walls with nine panels, each panel bearing an emblem. Thus, the first king of the first dynasty will occupy the first panel in the first room. A beacon on a hill will tell how he was named 'Phar-a-mond,' according to the system of Pâris. By Allevy's method, in placing above a mirror, which stands for 4, a bird 2 and a hoop 0, one will obtain 420, the date of that prince's accession."

Now mark the heroism of their total commitment, suffering all their surroundings to dissolve into a vast mnemonotechnic edifice:

> For greater clearness, they took, as a mnemonic base, their own house, where they were living, attaching to each one of its parts a distinct event—and the courtyard, the garden, the surroundings, the entire district, had no other meaning than to jog their memory. The boundary-posts in the country limited certain epochs, the apple-trees were genealogical trees, the bushes were battles, the world became a symbol.

It is the sacramental universe of the new learning, run up in a fortnight. "They sought, on the walls, a quantity of things that were not there, and ended by seeing them, but no longer knew the dates they represented."

But as the wave topples, watch them snatch truth from the wreck of method; for even as they lose hold on the means of recalling dates, they learn that the dates themselves are not worth recalling:

> Besides, dates are not always authentic. They learnt, in a student's manual, that the date of the birth of Jesus must be put back five years earlier than is usual, that with the Greeks there were three ways of reckoning the Olympiads, and with the Romans eight ways of dating the beginning of the year. So many opportunities for mistakes, besides those that result from the signs of the zodiac, eras, and different sorts of calendars.
>
> And from disregard of dates they passed to contempt for facts.
>
> What is important is the philosophy of history.

This in turn they speedily discard; and having exhaustively proved the total impossibility of writing history, they set out to write one.

So much in three pages, less than one per cent of the book; never was zeal so disinterested, so unflagging. Weaving ropes of sand and carving monuments in water, they undo with fantastic thoroughness the work of 3,000 years, dismembering Solomon's house stone by stone and bringing the New Atlantis level with the waves, during thirty years (thirty years!) sojourn inside the world of the Encyclopaedia, where most of us have not the heart to venture for more than a few minutes at a time. At seventy-five they are as dauntless as at fifty. Their very despairs—as when they arrive at the certainty that nothing exists—are but stages of the illuminative way, "into the desolation of reality." And when all else has failed; when they have plumbed to the uttermost the follies of a hundred systems; discarded

agriculture, arboriculture and formal gardening;
chemistry, medicine, astronomy, archaeology and geology;
prehistory, history and the philosophy of history;
literature, grammar and aesthetics;
politics;
love, gymnastics;
mesmerism, magnetism, spiritualism and the evocation of the dead;
metaphysics, suicide, Christianity, even Buddhism;

why then, having retraced the history of the human race from the tilling of the fields to theology the queen of sciences and seen all these crumble to dust, then still dauntless they take up pedagogy, so that they may reclaim two waifs from brutality and instill in them the love of learning. Odysseus himself was less heroic; he was succored by the memory of an Ithaca he had known.

Yet it seems clear that Pécuchet and his friend Bouvard lack the ideal qualifications for their high calling; for one thing, they are both getting old. They are just old enough, however, for Flaubert's purposes, and born moreover, according to their author's careful determinations, precisely in the nick of time to inherit the ages. For their great experiment commences toward the end of 1840, when each of them has lived half a hundred years; which means that they were born in the first months of the new heaven and the new earth, about 1790, when the Revolution had decreed the obsolescence of cant, superstition and custom. Like Russians born in the year 1918, they are untainted by the least memory of a time when knowledge, which is power, was the preserve of the few. Their very life in the womb commenced after the fall of the Bastille, and was transacted in utter innocence of clerical tyranny or the insolence of hereditary office.

"Memories almost their own," we are told, enlivened accounts of "the highroads covered with soldiers singing the Marseillaise. On the doorsteps sat women sewing the canvas for the tents. Sometimes there came a stream of men in red caps, carrying on the end of a slanted pike a bloodless head with hanging locks. The lofty tribune of the Convention towered above a cloud of dust, where enraged faces were howling cries of death. As one passed at midday near the lake of the Tuileries, one heard the shock of the guillotine, as though sheep were being axed."

Of all this, contemporaneous with their infancy, they are the inheritors, so that in the summer of 1845 they shudder under no tyranny, but take their ease in the garden, under the arbor, savoring the freedom to know. "Pécuchet, with a little stool beneath his feet, was reading aloud in his hollow voice, tirelessly, and only stopping to plunge his fingers in his snuff-box. Bouvard was listening to him with his pipe in his mouth, his legs apart, the top of his trousers unbuttoned."

For if there is one thing certain about the Enlightenment it is this, that the Revolution has democratized its benefits, and released, for any pair of copying-clerks, the assurances, the freedom for the intellect to play, that were once monopolies of the salon. And this is a capital fact, that Flaubert locates their enterprise so exactly at the semicentenary of civilization's new frontier, like a solemn commemorative ritual. Every man is at liberty now to be his own polymath. The mind of Europe has disclosed its secret contents and become a vast Coney Island in which all France is entitled to play.

And are they not all France? They are all France's notion of all France. Flaubert, the great connoisseur of received ideas, does not omit to register the most pervasive idea of all, that Frenchmen are by turns sensual and rational; worldly, lecherous and suave, or else rigorous, logical, prickly; the fat and the thin, the optimist and the pessimist; the Mediterranean and the Roman temperament, respectively. In dividing this vast cliche neatly into its elements, he commenced with their names, by which he set great store: Bouvard, a full round sound for the lips to caress; Pécuchet, crackling with the percussives of disciplined enunciation. And their full names, each once recorded, each an absurd thundering litany of emblems and rallying-cries: François Denys Bartholomée Bouvard; Juste Romain Cyrille Pécuchet! See how Rome and la Belle France answer one another: Juste Romain Cyrille—justice, Roman law, and a saint celebrated (says the *Encyclopaedia Britannica*) for his "furious zeal"; François Denys Bartholomée—France, the patron saint of France, and the apostle with the most orotund name of all, whose Day, moreover, is intertwined with the most intimate processes of pre-Revolutionary French history.[1] Of so much past do they bear the stamp; the one, therefore, "confident, irresponsible, open-handed; the other cautious, thoughtful, sparing."

All this has the mad precision of farce; and farce, sure enough, supplies the decor of page one. The empty street is described like an empty stage: "Lower down, the Canal St. Martin, enclosed by two locks, showed the straight line of its inky water. Midway, there was a boat filled with timber, and on the banks two rows of barrels." Two men appear, simultaneously, from opposite sides, one tall, one short; one plump, one stringy; the hair of one curly blond, of the other straight and black. They reach the middle of the boulevard, and as if on cue sit down simultaneously on

[1] Here I am in Vivian Mercier's debt, for pointing out these extraordinary names.

the same bench. And as if on cue, the machinery of recognition commences:

> In order to wipe their brows they removed their headgear, which each placed by his side; and the smaller man saw written in his neighbor's hat, "Bouvard"; while the latter easily made out in the cap of the individual wearing the frock-coat the word "Pécuchet."
> "Fancy that," he said. "We've both had the idea of writing our names in our hats."
> "Good heavens, yes; mine might be taken at the office."
> "The same with me; I work in an office too."

So insidiously plausible is this encounter that we are hardly sure whether we are in the domain of burlesque or not.

But burlesque of what? Why, of fiction. For behind that half-page we are to imagine a writer racking his brains for a plausible way to get the story started; we are to imagine the fussing over point of view; the agonizing over probabilities, since your French bourgeois does not, without some occasion, simply start talking to a total stranger; the wrestling with the sequence in which the characters are to be named, described, and set talking. We are to fancy (to transpose into modern terms) Jamesian beginnings, Faulknerian beginnings; the 500-word draft crumpled in a melodrama of despair; the 8,000-word draft composed, pruned, retouched, ripped up; the half-written circuitous opening, with its easy meditations on chance and destiny, never completed; the dismal brooding; and the joy. For in a transport of joy our author has realized with what efficiency he can manage the recognition scene if only each character does something on which the other may remark; and what more plausible than the doffed hat; and what better calculated to promote the doffed hat from plausibility to certainty than a temperature of 90 degrees (precisely 33 degrees Centigrade; odd numbers look more authentic). And to ensure that the doffed hat initiates talk, let there be something written inside it (masterstroke!); and to kill more than one bird with this pellet, let exposition be combined with mechanism, and let what is written inside the hat be the wearer's name. For otherwise, the characters would have to volunteer their names, and it is difficult to devise a way of managing this.

Or perhaps we are to imagine nothing of this sort; but to imagine instead a writer of demotic cunning, by nature so perfectly attuned to idiocy that his imagination, the moment it is set the problem of introducing two characters, spontaneously stages the scene in this way. For postulate a mind which functions out of habit on a certain plane of plausible unreality, the plane for example on which the business of detective novelettes is transacted, and it will be effortlessly fecund in such devices for maneuvering personages and information over the page.

At any rate, this is what was concocted for us, in August 1874, by the most meticulous craftsman of prose fiction the world had ever seen, the man for whom a tale of provincial adultery had been the labor of five years. "I flounder," he wrote six days after beginning the writing of *Bouvard,* "I flounder, I erase, I despair. Last night I was violently sick to my stomach. But it will go forward; it *must* go forward! The difficulties of this work are petrifying. No matter; by hard labor I can vanquish them." And petrifying they were; for the task he had set for himself was nothing less than to achieve by labor effects comparable to those of appalling incompetence: the incompetence that supposes the mirror held up to nature when two lay figures seat themselves simultaneously and take off in synchrony their hats: the incompetence, in short, of fiction itself, which is endlessly *arranging* things. He will use fiction itself to vanquish fiction; he will arrange, and maneuver, and contrive, to such bland effect that no one will ever afterward be quite sure where contrivance began and serendipity left off. He will use with cunning every device of the merely facile novelist; and the result will be such a compendium of unreality that it will seem real.

What happens, then, when the timeless pair have completed their exchange on hats? Why, what would happen? thinks the skilled hack. They would look into each other's faces; and this is plainly our cue for personal descriptions, which Sir Walter Scott inserted so awkwardly (but we know better now). And so:

> Then they inspected one another.
> Bouvard's pleasant appearance quite charmed Pécuchet.
> His blue eyes, always half closed, smiled out of a rosy face. His trousers, buttoning at the side and wrinkling down over buckskin shoes, took the shape of his stomach. . . .

and such are the resources of literary skill, we divine immediately that Bouvard is fat. These are sophisticated times; once Bouvard would have been introduced as the stout man. It is the same with the conversation that soon commences:

> Suddenly a drunken man zigzagged across the pavement, and they began a political discussion on the subject of the working classes. Their opinions were alike, except that Bouvard was perhaps more liberal-minded.

Or,

> The sight of this wedding-party led Bouvard and Pécuchet to talk of women, whom they declared flighty, perverse

and obstinate. All the same, they were often better than men; though at other times they were worse. In short, it was best to live without them; and Pécuchet had remained single.

Or later, when the prostitute has strutted by with the soldier,

. . . Bouvard indulged in a smutty remark. Pécuchet grew very red and, doubtless to avoid replying, indicated with a glance that a priest was approaching.

The ecclesiastic stalked down the avenue of thin young elms that studded the pavement, and when the three-cornered hat was out of sight Bouvard expressed his relief, for he hated Jesuits. Pécuchet, without absolving them altogether, showed some respect for religion.

We are given barely ten words of their dialogue; we can reconstruct it, though, with ease. Our reconstruction will depend on the prime convention of commercial fiction: that there is a little stock of standard dialogues on given subjects—politics, domesticity, religion—which the reader by this time knows as well as the author; and that a drunken man is a political object, a wedding party a domestic object, and a priest a religious object, the mere sight of which will initiate the dialogue appropriate to it. Flaubert, busily at work behind this subversive enterprise of his, is leaving us the blanks to fill in, by way of making three points: (1) that we know how to fill them in; hence (2) that prose fiction consists of standard passages which the reader soon learns to negotiate as he does a familiar stairway; and (3) that the dimmest novel cannot compete, in obviousness, with middle-class life itself, middle-class life in which people exchange responses a Flaubert can calculate with Newtonian precision, and exchange these under the impression that they are making conversation, by which man is distinguished from the brutes.

And this completes the Flaubertian circle, which being a circle brings together irreconcilable extremes: actual life, gravid, numinous, authentic; and, jejune, simian, rampant in the abeyance of all but the contriving faculty, commercial literature. The hack writer it seems, he is the supreme realist.

III

Flaubert's patient aping of commercial formulas is of course not confined to *Bouvard et Pécuchet*. Consider the dialogue between Emma Bovary and Léon:

> "I think there is nothing so admirable as sunsets," she resumed, "but especially by the side of the sea."
> "Oh, I adore the sea!" said Monsieur Léon.
> "And then, does it not seem to you," continued Madame Bovary, "that the mind travels more freely on this limitless expanse, the contemplation of which elevates the soul, gives ideas of the infinite, the ideal?"

In the *Dictionnaire des Idées Reçues* for which Flaubert amassed material over some three decades, we find:

> MER: N'a pas de fond. Image de l'infini.—Donne des grandes pensées.

A page later Emma has reached music:

> Emma continued: "And what music do you prefer?"
> "Oh, German music; that which makes you dream."

GUSTAVE FLAUBERT: *Comedian of the Enlightenment*

Again their conversation echoes the *Dictionnaire:*

> ALLEMANDS: Peuple de rêveurs (vieux).

Here, finally, are Emma and Léon on Poetry:

> "Has it ever occurred to you," Léon went on, "to come across some vague idea of your own in a book, some dim image that comes back to you from afar, and as the completest expression of your own slightest sentiment?"
>
> "I have experienced it," she replied.
>
> "That is why," he said, "I especially love the poets. I think verse more tender than prose, and that it moves far more easily to tears."
>
> "Still in the long run it is tiring," continued Emma. "Now I, on the contrary, adore stories that rush breathlessly along, that frighten me. I detest commonplace heroes and moderate sentiments, such as there are in nature."
>
> "In fact," observed the clerk, "these works, not touching the heart, miss, it seems to me, the true end of art. It is so sweet, amid all the disenchantments of life, to be able to dwell in thought among noble characters, pure affections, and pictures of happiness. . . ."

This happens not to echo the *Dictionnaire,* the entries in which, when they pertain to Literature or Poetry, are of the most curt and impatient description. It is easy to identify the kind of thing it does echo: it is a veritable checklist of things it is fashionable to think about literary enchantment. It is not, in fact, a really convincing bit of dialogue, so aware are we of the author's checklist. Emma and Léon are meant to be talking completely out of books, and Flaubert's dialogue is at its best when the books are at a little distance.

This is the unfailing charm of the *Dictionnaire des Idées Reçues,* that the books lie generally at a distance. The ideas there conveniently codified have been *reçues*—received, accepted—because of their inherent resonance with the honest middle-class soul, *anima naturaliter inepta.* "Vox populi, vox Dei," runs its portentous subtitle; and in 1850, the very year in which he was much later to place Bouvard and Pécuchet's speculations on the Social Contract and the Divine Right, he was explaining to a correspondent, how this book, "equipped with a fine preface to show how it was undertaken in order to guide the public back to tradition, order, and convention, and so arranged that the reader could never be sure if he was being made a fool of or not," had in fact a good chance of success; "car elle serait toute d'actualité." This "Catalogue des idées chic" admits different sorts of material, the author never having quite delimited its scope. Some of the entries reflect his private irritations; we can imagine the savagery with which he noted "PROSE: Easier to write than verse." Some reflect simple fatigue with the thing too often said: "FUNERAL: Of the deceased: And to think that I had dinner with him only a week ago!" Some codify medical lore: "NIGHTMARE: Comes from the stomach." But it is when it touches on the rhetoric of bourgeois omniscience that the conception grows transcendent. Thus of "EXTIRPATE" we are told that this verb is used only of heresies and corns, and of "ERECTION" that it is used only of monuments. Whether these remarks are descriptive or prescriptive we cannot tell. "MALEDICTIONS" are "given only by fathers." "MESSAGE" is "more noble than letter." "IVORY" is used only of teeth, and "ALABASTER" of "the finest parts of the female body." And honest indignation makes for its target with untrammeled certainty. Certain things are to inspire our indignation: "s'indigner contre:" waltzes, for example, and New Year's gifts.

GUSTAVE FLAUBERT: *Comedian of the Enlightenment*

Others, a notch higher, we are to fulminate against: Flaubert's fine idiom is "tonner contre," though of FULMINER he remarks, "joli verbe." "Tonner contre" is the order whenever we are confronted with, for instance, the Baccalaureate, the Cuisine of the Midi, Duelling, Sybarites, Eclecticism and "EPOQUE (la nôtre)." At least twice, Flaubert brings our capacity for indignation to untranslatable apotheosis. Of HIATUS we receive his categorical imperative, "ne pas le tolerer." And as for the Pyramids, cunningly exploiting the placement of the French adjective to apotheosize Johnson's meditation on one stone to no purpose laid upon another, he levels them with a single blast of republican scorn: "PYRAMIDE: Ouvrage inutile."

The idea of arranging such things alphabetically came to Flaubert as early as 1843. Alphabetical arrangement suggests at once a useful book, a guide to conversation as the usual Dictionary is a guide to writing. We confront at once this difficulty, however, that when you are writing you can stop to look up words and no one will be the wiser, whereas when you are conversing it is hardly *comme il faut* to be referring constantly to a handbook as various subjects present themselves. We have thus the most useless useful book imaginable, since it is precisely when you need it that you cannot possibly consult it. So there inheres in the very conception a sort of Heisenberg's Principle, and a Platonic characterization of the supreme bourgeois, the very *Idea* of a bourgeois, equipped with this work in which he has invested a portion of his capital, but which can only benefit him on some pure plane of theory where the act of conversing is as abstract and timeless as the act of writing an Encyclopaedia article. So the first thing that the alphabetical arrangement does is plunge the entire work into absurdity. The second thing it does is supply just the discontinuity of surface that gave Flaubert such trouble in writing prose, permuting with dreary labor the three forms of the French past tense, balancing period against epigram, narrative with reflection. And the third thing we gather from the alphabetical arrangement is the scientific character of the work; it is finally, says M. Descharmes,

> a sheaf of notes to which Flaubert has distilled his psychological and moral observations, the stupidities he heard repeated all around him, the characteristic gestures of people in given circumstances, all the lacunae and all the pretensions of cautious good sense, of bourgeoisdom in its most general form.[2]

For Art, Flaubert wrote to George Sand, is not meant to portray exceptions; like Science itself, it is meant to portray things as they *always* are, in themselves, in their general nature, disengaged from all ephemeral contingency; and each article in the *Dictionary,* M. Descharmes notes, is the synthesized result of an indefinite number of particular observations, isolated presentations, phrases repeated on the same subject by people of different social and intellectual classes. Each definition supposes a vast documentation, amassed during years of patient listening.

It is therefore, finally, a handbook for novelists; Art tending toward the general and human behavior tending toward the cliche, we are back again to the fact that the supreme artist is the cliche expert and cannot do better than to imitate, as closely as he can, the procedures of the hack. If the *Dictionary* is useless for guiding conversation, it is useful for the writer; and the writer who used it was Flaubert himself, turning, it would seem from entry to entry precisely like a correspondence-school novelist. It was one

[2] See René Descharmes, *Autour de Bouvard et Pécuchet,* Paris, 1921.

of the tenets of the Enlightenment, that Art can be systematized, its long traditions having yielded a store of images and turns of phrase which we cannot do better than imitate. In the *Spectator* for May 28, 1711, there appeared an advertisement for a book of which three editions had sold out: "The Art of English Poetry, containing, I. Rules for making Verses. II. A Collection of the most natural, agreeable and sublime Thoughts, viz. Allusions, Similes, Descriptions and Characters of Persons and Things that are to be found in the best English Poets. III. A Dictionary of Rhymes." It is true that Flaubert's own *Dictionnaire* contains under DICTIONARY the entry, "Put together only for the ignorant," and under DICTIONARY OF RHYMES, "S'en servir? honteux!" But he himself, on causing Bouvard to awaken from a deep slumber, would seem to have consulted his own compilation: "DORMIR (trop): épaissit le sang," and accordingly wrote, "Bouvard . . . was nervous on waking, since prolonged sleep may bring on apoplexy." Or, having Pécuchet lecture on Astronomy ("belle science très utile pour la marine"), Flaubert has him broach the topic by stating that sailors employ it on their voyages. Nor was it only *Bouvard and Pécuchet* that he composed in this way; M. Descharmes gives many pages of examples culled from *Madame Bovary* and *L'Éducation Sentimentale*, and intimates that he could have done the same for *Un coeur Simple* as well.

Once we have seen *Le Dictionnaire des Idées Reçues* as a scientific compilation, only gathered, unlike the eighteenth-century poets' manuals, from the life rather than from other books, we are in a position to notice a highly peculiar phenomenon, to which Flaubert pointed the way in proposing to publish the *Dictionnaire* itself as a book. For clothed in the authority of print, complete with an

Fig. 2   Flaubert digesting a newly received idea

elaborate Preface, it would serve to authorize what it had begun by merely collecting. To set before the middle classes exactly what they think and say, in codified form, is to establish a feedback loop, and feedback may have either a positive sign, encouraging the phenomena it transmits, or a negative, diminishing them. It pleased Flaubert to imagine a nation of readers no one of whom would ever dare open his mouth again, for fear of uttering one of the phrases the Dictionary contained. But the book would have depended, for its comic effect, on flirting with the other possibility, positive feedback, a gloriously efficient standardization of bourgeois behavior, confirmed, launched, invested in Print, bursting with confidence, fulminating as never before against Sybarites, Eclecticisme and Époque (la nôtre), or exchanging with now indestructible conviction its affirmations on Health (too much of it, cause of sickness), Homer (never existed; famous for his laughter) and Humidity (cause of all illness).

For already a surprising amount of this lore has leaked into the popular mind out of printed pages; the non-existence of Homer, for example, was a scholarly notion before it became the property of the Vox Populi. We may go further; Emma Bovary herself would have been impossible without books, quantities of books, books of the very sort that *Madame Bovary* itself approximates, and filled with dialogue very like her dialogues with her husband and her several lovers. *Madame Bovary* is a novel about a woman who has read novels, kept as close as possible to the plot, the characterization, and the dialogue of the sort of novels she has read.

IV

Once again we have returned to the center of the maze, where life and art are uncertain which copies the other. We note the continuity of Flaubert's themes; from first to last he is the great student of cultural feedback, writing books about what books do to the readers of books, one eye always on the sort of thing his own book is going to do to its own reader. We note too that in *Madame Bovary* the conception is still essentially primitive. Emma has transposed the themes and sentiments of novels into life, with the lack of success one might expect. Flaubert's narrative, that is, assigns causes; if the hack is the supreme realist, it may be because real people have been modeling their actions on the imaginative products of hacks. Certainly, for the *Dictionary* entries on which he based the discourses of Emma and Léon, Flaubert need not have listened to thousands of Emmas and Léons; he could have gotten "Sea: image of the infinite" directly out of other novels, and perhaps did.

In *Bouvard et Pécuchet*, however, there is no question of making a scapegoat out of second-rate fiction. On the contrary, as we have seen, the book itself aspires *directly* to the idiot accuracy of second-rate fiction. The two heroes, furthermore, aspire directly to the utter insanities of scientific genius. We have not before us a travesty of anything. We have the thing itself. We hear of them, for example, checking by experiment the assertion that animal heat is developed by muscular contraction. Bouvard enters a tepid bath, armed with a thermometer . . .

> "Move your limbs!" said Pécuchet.
> He moved them without any effect on the temperature.
> "It's decidedly cold."

GUSTAVE FLAUBERT: *Comedian of the Enlightenment*

"I'm not warm myself," replied Pécuchet, also starting to shiver. "But work your pelvic members! Make them stir!"

Bouvard opened his thighs and waggled his buttocks, rocked his stomach, puffed like a whale, then looked at the thermometer, which all the time was falling.

"I can't make it out; yet my limbs are moving."

"Not enough."

And he went on with his gymnastics.

He keeps this up for three hours, while the thermometer falls to 53 degrees.

This seems imbecilic; but certainly, if the temperature of the bath had risen, even fractionally, they would not seem imbecilic at all; they would have been the co-discoverers of Bouvard's Law. Equal absurdity menaced the researches of the man who inserted brass wires into the spinal marrow of dead frogs, and allowed their feet to touch an iron plate, to see if the dead legs would move. But they did move, and the phenomenon was called Galvanism, and Charlotte Brontë was enabled to write of a melancholy hero that the heroine's approach "always galvanized him into a new and spasmodic life"; so Galvani and his dead frog contributed to literature as well as to science.

That Bouvard and Pécuchet are easily dismissed as absurd just because they fail is a highly important principle. Aesthetically considered, Galvani with his dead frogs, all hanging by brass hooks from an iron wire, their legs twitching in concert, is equally absurd, irremediably absurd, dismally open to the charge that man created in God's image is on this occasion passing his time in a very strange way. It is facts that are absurd; nothing is more absurd than the very conception of a *fact*, an isolated datum of experience, something to find out, isolated from all the other things that there are to be found out; the twitch, under certain conditions, of a dead frog's legs, or the presence, in an optimum Galvanic Battery, of thirty pieces of silver. Before encyclopaedias were invented, facts had to be invented, the very concept of a fact: fact as the atom of experience, for the encyclopaedist to set in its alphabetical place, in dramatic testimony to the realization that no one knows in what other place to set it, or under what circumstances it may be wanted again. The N.E.D. does not find the word "fact" used in this way before 1632. Before then, a fact was a thing done, *factum,* part of a continuum of deed and gesture.

And it is facts, at last, that Flaubert sets out to wither. The critic Anthony Thorlby has described very well how Flaubert isolates detail from detail to this end:

> Each fact is isolated in turn, with sufficient detachment from the next to emphasize the absence of any real perspective between one kind of fact and another. And since facts presented all from the same point of view inevitably fall into some kind of perspective and assume a real meaning as a whole, this has required a constant interruption of stylistic continuity, by means of change in tense, person, subject, tone, direct and reported speech, and whatever other device of syntax and vocabulary Flaubert could muster. That is why virtually every phrase set him a new problem in expression: how to turn it aesthetically to bring out its essential sameness as a fact.[3]

For he is busily reproducing in a fabulous narrative the inanity of the Encyclopaedia; and Mr. Thorlby ends by comparing the whole heroic book to "an immensely complex and comprehensive mathematical formula which makes everything equal zero."

[3] Anthony Thorlby, *Gustave Flaubert,* Yale University Press, 1957, p. 54.

GUSTAVE FLAUBERT: *Comedian of the Enlightenment*

Scholars and thinkers have been butts of satire ever since Aristophanes disclosed Socrates suspended in a basket, to bring him nearer the clouds. It is not, however, with facts that the comic Socrates trifles, since the very notion of a fact is not to be invented for 2,000 years. He trifles with Reason, making the worse argument appear the better. By the time of the next great academic satire, the third book of *Gulliver's Travels,* humanity has encountered Facts; indeed Gulliver's mind is totally given over to fact, and so is the ant-like energy of Swift's prose, moving crumbs of information hither and thither with an activity exactly proportioned to their magnitude. The scientists in Lagado, however, are not, for better or worse, preoccupied with Facts but with Projects. Swift ridicules their activities, not their methods: their proposals to extract sunlight from cucumbers, or food from excrement, seeking to reverse the direction of processes that have flowed in their present direction since the world was made, with the inevitability of great rivers. These people are doing something foolish; it remains open to learning to do things that are wise. Another century and a half, however, and Flaubert will be suggesting that nothing remains open to learning at all, nothing but the cataloguing of its own inanities.

Having failed to lead their pupils Victor and Victorine into paths of virtue and contemplation, Bouvard and Pécuchet determine on schemes of adult education, so grandiose that their speedy ruin brings total disgrace; and everything having come to pieces in their hands, they resolve to copy as in the old days. So, at a two-seated desk, specially constructed, Flaubert meant them to live out their days, side by side, making up out of all the books that they have read what can best be described as an Encyclopaedia. Hear Descharmes' description of the unwritten second volume:

Fig. 3   *Bouvard playing Phèdre*

They would copy above all for the pleasure of copying, and the high comedy of their labor they would doubtless never suspect. Thence would come peace, even intellectual tranquillity, for this mechanical labor would serve to disentangle the confusion of their ideas, to classify the contradictory notions with which their narrow minds buzz, to supply them with ready-made judgments, generally vouched for by some authoritative name. And in their inexhaustible desire to learn, they would make daily additions to this *Encyclopédie grotesque* with further reading and new annotations, happy at last to be safe from the perils of putting theory into practice, and to be storing up, with no notion of using it, an archive of misdirected learning.

Here the serpent commences to swallow his tail; for *Bouvard and Pécuchet* was at last to commence displaying, in ordered form, its own vast materials, distilled from Flaubert's 11,000 pages of notes. It is a book made of facts, and facts reduced, by every artifice Flaubert could devise, to an extraordinary blank plane of autonomous factuality; and it was finally to spew forth again its own sources, summarized, digested, annotated. Under CONTRADICTIONS, we should have read seven opinions on the time it takes a body to putrefy completely, ranging from forty years to fifteen months; under BELLES IDÉES, Bernardin St. Pierre's statement that the melon was divided into slices by nature to facilitate its consumption by families; under ANECDOTES the case history of a Marine Officer's twenty years' constipation; and under I do not know what heading, the declaration of the Bishop of Metz, in December 1846, that the floods of the Loire in that year were due to the excesses of the Press and the imperfect observation of the Sabbath.

So fact, 11,000 pages of fact, having buttressed fiction,

fiction was at length to issue in fact, the very characters in the novel perfecting and completing their author's researches. So, with the classic simplicity which like everything classic verges on the banal, the clerks were to come full circle, copying as they had begun by copying, and the generic novel full circle, a cliche of plot superintending their immense amassement of cliches. So the scientific character of the novel, its quest for the ideal type, the general law, was to turn upon itself like a haruspex scrutinizing his own entrails. And so, finally, the intellectual progress of the human race was to be completed in miniature during the thirty-odd years of Bouvard and Pécuchet's researches; for having commenced, like the Greeks, heroic men, nearly mythological in their zeal, a new Cadmus, a new Pisistratus, they were to finish like neo-Christians, monastic men, in a new dark ages of the intellect, side by side at their manuscripts, sifting, preserving; and having commenced, like the first men, tilling the fields, they were to end like the last men, making Encyclopaedias: inheriting, so, the new heaven and the new earth of the Enlightenment.

2. *James Joyce:*

COMEDIAN OF THE INVENTORY

I

FLAUBERT, we know, was the connoisseur of the *mot juste*, lifted with tweezers from its leatherette box by a lapidary of choleric diligence. Paragraph after paragraph, page after page, his scores of special-purpose words certify, by their very air of uniqueness, to a resolute artistry for which stock parts would not suffice. His tight, burnished set pieces slacken considerably in translation; if we want to see something in English that resembles them, we cannot do better than consult *Ulysses,* where Bloom's cat "blinked up out of her avid shameclosing eyes," or "Frail from the housetops two plumes of smoke ascended, pluming, and in a flaw of softness softly were blown," or "Two shafts of soft daylight fell across the flagged floor from the high barbicans; and at the meeting of their rays a cloud of coalsmoke and fumes of fried grease floated, turning."

Such sentences, while they contain no difficulty of reference or content, might send a foreign reader to his dictionary, whether to find out the meaning of such words as "avid" and "barbicans," which while not recherche fall well outside a basic English vocabulary, or else to make sure that his difficulty in fitting less uncommon words together is not due to their possessing meanings of which he is unaware. Like Flaubert, Joyce in such passages throws the words into isolation, exposing their unmortared surfaces; when he assimilates them into idioms it is because he wants us to notice the idiom, which is commonly a borrowing or a parody.

It is by imagining the difficulties of a foreign reader that we can most readily see Joyce's characteristic way of dealing with the single word. For he continuously evades the normal English patterns to which structural linguists have devoted so much study. He places the adverbial phrase before the object ("her fingertip lifted to her mouth random crumbs"), sets the verb between the subject and phrases in apposition to the subject ("Down stage he strode some paces, grave, tall in affliction, his long arms outheld"), and is tirelessly resourceful in placing the adverb where it will exert stress against the other members of the sentence. ("He passed, dallying, the windows of Brown Thomas, silk mercers.") These are not the maneuvers of a man speaking, but of a man writing: a man setting down twelve or fourteen selected words and determining in what order to arrange them. A man speaking arranges larger structural units than words. Frank Budgen recalls their discussion of what had been for Joyce a solid day's work: two sentences. "You have been seeking the *mot juste?*" "No," said Joyce, "I have the words already. What I am seeking is the perfect order of words in the sentence. There is an order in every way appropriate. I think I have it."

It is perfectly natural that *Ulysses* should have attracted the attention of a group of scholars who wanted practice in compiling a word-index to some extensive piece of prose. More than any other work of fiction, it suggests by its texture, often by the very look of its pages, that it has been painstakingly assembled out of single words, and that we may learn something by taking the words apart again and grouping them for alphabetical study. Thanks to Professor Miles Hanley and his collaborators, we therefore know exactly how many different words it contains (29,899); which one is used most often ("the"), and how many times (14,877); which, and how many (16,432), used once only. The Hanley Word-Index to *Ulysses*[1] simply carries to an extreme of thoroughness the sort of marginal cross-references every student of the book pencils on page after page of his copy.

For the reader of *Ulysses* holds a book in his hands. Homer envisaged no such possibility. Consider what it makes feasible. On page 488 we read, "Potato preservative against plague and pestilence, pray for us." Now just sixty pages earlier, if we were alert, we may have noted the phrase, "Poor mamma's panacea," murmured by Bloom as he feels his trouser pocket. And fully 372 pages before that, on the bottom line of page 56, we have Bloom feeling in his hip pocket for the latchkey and reflecting, "Potato I have." The serious reader's copy of *Ulysses* acquires cross-references at three points; and Bloom's potato, it is by now commonplace to remark, is but one trivial instance among hundreds of motifs treated very briefly at two or three widely separated points in the book, and not even intelligible until the recurrences have been collated. It is customary to note that Joyce makes very severe demands of his reader. To learn something new from this commonplace we have only to set down its corollary. The demands Joyce makes on the reader would be impossible ones if the

[1] Madison, Wisconsin, 1937.

Fig. 4 Joyce writing a sentence

reader did not have his hands on the book, in which he can turn to and fro at his pleasure. And more than that: the whole conception of *Ulysses* depends on the existence of something former writers took for granted as simply the envelope for their wares: a printed book whose pages are numbered.

II

Any book so conceived has broken with narrative, though it may go through certain forms of storytelling. Narrative implies that someone is talking. It is an art that unfolds its effects in time, like music. It holds us under the spell of a voice, or something analogous to a voice, and (again like music) it slowly gathers into a simplified whole in the memory. The supreme vividness of the present instant blends continually with times gone: words fade, past scenes blur, scenes and characters we had forgotten reappear with studied eclat in some late phase of the adventure; the voice presses on, and the effect is completed as the final words set up resonances among our recollections of all that has preceded. No one understood this better than Joseph Conrad, who is at such pains to subject us to the spell of the teller of a tale. Conrad, with his studied apparatus of spoken narrative discharged into a reflective silence, attempted to carry to some ideal limit the convention under which Dickens, for instance, had operated with such confidence: the convention that a tale is something told, an act of intrepidity on the part of the teller, who is venturing where he has really never been before; and that the tale is a whole only in the hearer's memory; and that the written book is simply a record of the telling, or purports to be such a record. If we press back to Dickens we find an even simpler convention: the written book is a script, to be brought to life in oral delivery, by some middle-class Englishman reading aloud at his fireside, or by the author on an American tour. Far back of Dickens, again, lies Homer, whose book is simply a graph of what the bard recited: something that lived exactly in his memory, and gets transferred to the listener's memory less exactly. A manuscript or printed book, entitled *The Odyssey,* has simply this function, that it takes the place of the rhapsode's memory, somewhat deadly, somewhat mechanically.

Homer, of course, also lies behind *Ulysses;* and the most profound of all Joyce's Homeric transformations is this, that the text of *Ulysses* is not organized in memory and unfolded in time, but both organized and unfolded in what we may call *technological space:* on printed pages for which it was designed from the beginning. The reader explores its discontinuous surface at whatever pace he likes; he makes marginal notes; he turns back whenever he chooses to an earlier page, without destroying the continuity of something that does not press on, but will wait until he resumes. He is maneuvered, in fact, precisely into the role of the scholiasts whose marginalia encumbered the Alexandrian manuscripts of Homeric texts; only here is a text designed, as Homer's was not, precisely for this sort of study. It really *does* contain, as Homer's work was reputed to contain, a systematic compendium of arts, sciences and moral teachings; symbols, rituals and practical counsels; Irish history and the geography of the city of Dublin. If we are agreed that Homer's text does not designedly contain all the things that symbolic exegesis used to find there, it is because we are convinced that Homer spoke and sang but did not fuss over a manuscript. The Alexandrian scholars lived in a manuscript culture, whose conventions they

JAMES JOYCE: *Comedian of the Inventory*

projected onto their author. Joyce, however, did fuss over a manuscript, and a manuscript designed for a printer, and he pored over galley proofs and page proofs also. Joyce is acutely aware that the modern Homer must deal with neither an oral culture nor a manuscript one, but with a culture whose shape and whose attitude to its daily experience is determined by the omnipresence of the printed book.

He was very careful, therefore, to reproduce in his text the very quality of print, its reduction of language to a finite number of interchangeable and permutable parts. We have the impression, as we read the Circe episode, that we have encountered all its ingredients before, only in a different arrangement.

> Dennis Breen, whitetallhatted, with Wisdom Hely's sandwich-board, shuffles past them in carpet slippers, his dull beard thrust out, muttering to right and left. Little Alf Bergan, cloaked in the pall of the ace of spades, dogs him to left and right, doubled in laughter.

This combines Mr. Breen, the Mad Hatter's hat, the sandwichmen from page 152, a shuffling gait and the phrase "dull beard" from page 157, Breen's dream of the ace of spades from page 155, and Alf Bergan who on page 157 is named as the probable sender of a disturbing postcard. (This is a hasty census: I may have missed a few items.) There presides over this phantasmagoria precisely the faith that presides over the eighteenth century's rationalism, the faith that we can register all relevant phenomena in some book where we can find them again: in a dictionary, where human speech is dissociated into words which can be listed in alphabetical order, or in an encyclopaedia, where human knowledge is broken up into discontinuous fragments to be registered on a similar principle.

The Rev. Walter J. Ong, S.J., has argued brilliantly that printing was the efficient cause of those intellectual movements which in the sixteenth and seventeenth centuries destroyed the hierarchies of knowledge and rearranged the things we know for the sake of pedagogic convenience. Certainly it was printing which led us to think of speech as being composed of interchangeable parts, if only because printing and its by-product lexicography enforced a uniformity of spelling which gave each separate word a stable identity to the eye, whatever its equivocal status for the ear. After that, writing becomes a matter of locating and arranging words, as Joyce spent his celebrated day trying out different arrangements of fifteen words:

"Perfume of embraces all him assailed. With hungered flesh obscurely, he mutely craved to adore."

Those words he caused to lie within the gestures of the spoken voice, while conveying tensions that speech, which manipulates phrases rather than words, would never have discovered for itself.

Printing also leads to the manufacture of books, and to the nuisance of untalented authors. And here we encounter one of those loops in time, uniting the eighteenth and the twentieth centuries, which the student of Joyce's Dublin learns to anticipate, welcome, and explore. For the first author of talent to have been forcibly struck by the *nature* of the printed book appears to have been a compatriot of Joyce's and a great denizen of *Finnegans Wake,* by name Jonathan Swift.

III

There are many ways of describing *A Tale of a Tub;* let us call it one thing more, a parody of the book as a book.

JAMES JOYCE: *Comedian of the Inventory*

For its method is to emphasize to the point of grotesqueness exactly those features which distinguish the printed book *per se,* the printed book a technological artifact, from a human document. Human documents Swift is prepared to understand, though looking around him in 1704 or thereabouts, in the first dawn of the bookseller's paradise, he can discern precious few.

Between a human document and the thing that Gutenberg's monster typically disgorges, a distinction may be discovered which turns on the intimate nature of what the brain thinks and the hand writes. For Swift, a piece of writing is properly something that exists in a personal context, where one human being is seeking to gain the confidence and understanding of another. Pamphlets like the *Modest Proposal* or the *Argument Against Abolishing Christianity* depend for their effect on our understanding and approving this fact: their supposed author reposes in a state of bland rapport with readers who will respond suitably to his insinuations and share his notions of rational conduct. Though the pamphlet is anonymous, its effect is not to efface the supposed author but to generalize him; he is the obedient humble servant of whatever reader is jackass enough to find him congenial. The rapport between them, while it depraves the rational intercourse of honest men, is still an intercourse between persons: as much so, Swift might add, as an act of sodomy. By contrast Swift finds in the typical contemporary printed book no trace of the inviolable human person. *A Tale of a Tub* is not at bottom a civil letter, as a pamphlet is essentially a letter. It is anonymous because it is written by nobody, by no person, but by the autonomous book-compiling machine itself; and it addresses itself, like a public speech from the scaffold, to the public at large and to posterity—that is, to no one. *A Tale of a Tub* is the first comic exploitation of that technological space which the words in a large printed book tend to inhabit. Commerce and capital had recently discovered that printing is not simply a way of disseminating manuscripts, but that a book is an artifact of a new kind. This discovery brought with it a host of technical gimmicks which Swift regards with fascinated disquiet. We have discovered in the same way that the motion picture is not simply a way of recording plays, but a different medium; and that television is not simply a way of disseminating motion pictures, but a different medium; and each of these discoveries has brought with it an embarrassing swarm of new techniques. So it was, in Swift's day, with the book: and *A Tale of a Tub* is the register of Gutenberg technology, discerned by a man who regarded each of the bookmaker's devices as a monstrous affront to the personal intercourse which letters in a dialogue culture had served to promote.

The book as book entails, then, Introductions, Prefaces, Apologies and Dedications; Headings, Subheadings; Tables, Footnotes, Indices; even Pictures. The way in which some of these help mechanize the act of discourse is perfectly plain. Take the footnote, for instance.[2] The footnote's relation to the passage from which it depends is established wholly by visual and typographic means, and will typically defeat all efforts of the speaking voice to clarify it without visual aid. Parentheses, like commas, tell the voice what to do: an asterisk tells the voice that it can do nothing. You cannot read a passage of prose aloud, interpolating the footnotes, and make the subordination of the footnotes

[2] I do not mean the scholar's footnote which supplies a reference, but the footnote that supplements, qualifies, parallels, quips, digresses or elucidates.

clear,[3] and keep the whole sounding natural. The language has forsaken a vocal milieu, and a context of oral communication between persons, and commenced to take advantage of the expressive possibilities of technological space.

This ventriloqual gadget, the footnote, deserves some attention, partly because Swift became a great virtuoso on this new instrument, and Joyce later devoted a whole section of *Finnegans Wake* to ringing changes on the footnote and its cousin the marginalium. One would like to know when it was invented; it is as radical a discovery as the scissors or the rocking chair, and presumably as anonymous. The man who writes a marginal comment is conducting a dialogue with the text he is reading; but the man who composes a footnote, and sends it to the printer along with his text, has discovered among the devices of printed language something analogous with counterpoint: a way of speaking in two voices at once, or of ballasting or modifying or even bombarding with exceptions[4] his own discourse without interrupting it. It is a step in the direction of discontinuity: of organizing blocks of discourse simultaneously in space rather than consecutively in time. We encounter its finest flower in the immense scheme of annotation to the final edition of the *Dunciad Variorum,* a project in which it is customary to discern Swift's hand. *The Dunciad,* like *A Tale of a Tub,* is not only a satire against the abuses of the Gutenberg era, but an exploitation of technical devices made available by that era. Because print enables us to distinguish verse from prose at once by eye, we may here observe, page by page, an Attic column of verse standing on a thick pedestal of miscellaneous learn-

[3] And they are often less subordinated than counterpointed.

[4] Some footnotes of course seem totally unrelated to the point in the text at which they are appended. They suggest an art form like the refrains in Yeats' late poems.

ing. Or the verse plunges majestically forward amid a strangely orderly babel of commentaries, assailed at random by every fly in Grub Street. Very often the note is needed to complete a poetic effect; Mr. Empson has analyzed a famous instance of this. And Pope's intricate mosaic of allusions to other poems, it is pertinent to remark, depends for its witty precision on a prime assumption of the Dunces, namely that poetry is to be found exclusively in books, that the texts of past classics are as stable as mosaic tiles (having been quick-frozen by the printer), and that someone with fingernail scissors and a little bottle of paste can rearrange the general stock of literature to produce new beauties. The Dunces themselves, of course, do this all the time; Pope is always careful to imitate their every mannerism with insolent fidelity; and it is the easier to do because metrical varieties have become so standardized, like that standardization of machine-screw threads which today makes possible an international technology.

We called the footnote[5] a device for organizing units of discourse discontinuously in space rather than serially in time. The same is true of the Introductions, Dedications and Digressions with which the *Tale* is so lavishly equipped. They all of them instance and exploit the essential discontinuity of the book as book. The introductory matter expands to a heroic scale certain printers' conventions. A conventional heading in large capital letters suffices to legitimize the presence in a book of almost anything the author and bookseller choose: flattery of some patron, for instance, which we can incorporate into any book at all simply by heading it *Dedication*. Swift allows the eponymous author of the *Tale* to plume himself mightily on his own capacity for sheer miscellaneousness, and carries this

[5] In the middle of the previous paragraph. Please pay attention.

theme into the text itself by the device of interpolating immense Digressions, each headed "Digression" to prevent any earnest reader from supposing that he is losing the thread. The first section of the book proper (headed Section One: the Introduction) makes a great pother about the various conditions for the oral delivery of wisdom: from the pulpit, the stage itinerant, the scaffold and perhaps the bench; but nothing is clearer from the beginning of this book to the end than the fact that all conceivable modes of oral discourse are totally unrelated to it. The Digressions, indeed, treat not of speech or dialogue but of every aspect of bookmaking: notably indices, tables of contents, anthologies, compilations, the art of digression, the practice of criticism and the improvement of madness in the commonwealth.

Having mentioned Pope's witty precisions, we should mention Swift's in turn, for the two of them generate a stylistic curve which passes axially through *Ulysses* and *Finnegans Wake*. If their exactness of language pleases and surprises, it is by a sort of analogy with deft manufacture; we acknowledge as much when we apply a word like "precision," which in the twentieth century is a technological metaphor. The *mot juste* is a beauty we owe to the omnipresence of the printer, because oral delivery tends to blur it. Our interest in the *mot juste* is a function of our concern with the single word, its look, feel, weight, history, range, and denotation: a concern first fostered by the eighteenth-century interest in lexicography, which interest in turn belongs to the age of the book. A scholiast writing marginalia to the *Odyssey* may pause over a single word to consider how Homer is using it here; but a lexicographer abstracts it from all particular usage. Samuel Johnson may be described as the first writer to have examined individually in turn each of the words he employs, and without actually compiling dictionaries, writers have followed his example ever since. Certainly Joyce does. And in Johnson's lexicography there is crystallized an attitude to language already for half a century prevalent and dominant, sponsored by the concern of a whole society's intelligence with the production of printed books. (A word assembled from leaden cubes in a type case, as Father Ong has indicated, is already well on its way to being an interchangeable part.) When Pope writes of a heroic Dunce plunging into the Thames,

"Furious he dives, precipitately dull,"

we know that the word "precipitately" has received from Pope a kind of attention which the word "incarnadine" did not receive from Shakespeare. Pope's wit consists in the exactness with which the word's etymology is being re-enacted in the line. Swift in the same way, reflecting on the posthumous fame of authors, is careful to arrange each of his individual words, clearly defined, into scintillation and balance.

> . . . whether it is that fame, being a fruit grafted on the body, can hardly grow, and much less ripen, till the stock is in the earth, or whether she be a bird of prey, and is lured, among the rest, to pursuit after the scent of a carcass: or whether she conceives her trumpet sounds best and farthest when she stands on a tomb, by the advantage of a rising ground, and the echo of a hollow vault.

We hear "carcass" start out from among the ceremonious euphemisms of decease, and hear the smart "advantage" offset the Virgilian "echo," and hear "rising ground" paralleled by "hollow vault," and no blur surrounds any of these effects, etched with lexicographic clarity. The effect is quite different from the effect that a similar terminology might have in a sermon of Donne's, because it is queerly unrelated to oral delivery: an eerie life stirs among words that have been briskly laid out to fill categories and complete tropes, in the stunned neutrality of print. Each term snaps magnetically into its place in the inviolable whole; each sentence is leveled like a course of bricks. To contrast these smartly articulated figures of thought, each one displayed and delimited like a little algebraic calculation, with some Shakespearean image groping obscurely among the roots of language for its own bases of relevance:

". . . Witness this army of such mass and charge . . ." is to perceive the kind of clarity that works by analogies with visual clarity and with the fact that we have before us a page to look at, where the backward glance to the beginning of any phrase, clearly indicated by the punctuation, will confirm the accuracy of every epithet. This is the precision which Joyce inherited from the first heyday of the book, and exploited as no one had exploited it before, out of some conatural awareness of the nature of a civilization structured by print.

Though Leopold Bloom's knowledge, for example, most of it traceable to books, is extremely inexact, it never produces on us an effect of confusion. There is no loss of outline: perfectly distinct words, each clearly remembered, have simply gotten into the wrong categories, or else sentences of which the beginnings have been fixed in his memory are incomplete because he has forgotten the endings.

> Where was that chap I saw in that picture somewhere? Ah, in the dead sea, floating on his back, reading a book with a parasol open. Couldn't sink if you tried: so thick with salt. Because the weight of water, no, the weight of the body in

the water is equal to the weight of the. Or is it the volume is equal of the weight? It's a law something like that. Vance in high school cracking his finger-joints, teaching. The college curriculum. Cracking curriculum. What is weight really when you say the weight? Thirty-two feet per second, per second. Law of falling bodies; per second, per second. They all fall to the ground. The earth. It's the force of gravity of the earth is the weight.

Whatever the deficiencies of Bloom's understanding, there is no blur around any of these words, any more than around Swift's. The sentences do not achieve the formulations one might find in the physics textbooks Bloom is half remembering, but each word is clearly enunciated, and so far as lexicography can tell us, clearly understood. In fact the criterion of intellectual adequacy Bloom has inherited, the criterion to which he does not succeed in living up (and who could?), is a criterion based on the authority of the book. One is not expected to understand the phenomena; one is expected to get the formulas right, to lay hold of all the words and arrange them in the order in which the textbook arranges them. This proposition is easily tested: observe that we do not need to understand the physical laws involved to be sure that Bloom does not understand them. We need only note the incompleteness of his sentences, and their bathetic, anticlimactic rhythms. For words are interchangeable parts to be arranged, and there are authorized arrangements the recitation of which evinces confidence. Stephen Dedalus may understand what he is talking about or he may not, but he enjoys the confidence of the born word-man: "Ineluctable modality of the visible: at least that if no more, thought through my eyes. Signatures of all things I am here to read, seaspawn and seawrack, the nearing tide, that rusty boot."

JAMES JOYCE: *Comedian of the Inventory*

That these examples touch principles which underlie the whole conception of *Ulysses,* is a fact obscurely recognized by the very large amount of critical energy that has been devoted to making wordlists for Joyce's books. The books, it is felt, are permutations of a stock of words which can be counted, enumerated, and classified. You can of course count, enumerate and classify Shakespeare's words, if you are so minded, but you are unlikely to attach any importance to the fact that a given word occurs in the canon, say, seven times. Or if you do attach importance to this fact, as the scholars do who explore Shakespeare's image-clusters, you will explain the fact on psychological grounds rather than assign it to deliberate technique. One does not think of Shakespeare as a man conscious that certain words, a large but finite number of them, enjoyed a proper existence, whereas any other words that came to his fancy were coinages. Joyce on the other hand, in a world where the dictionary and the printing press suggest limits to the authorized vocabulary, functions with a peculiar sardonic awareness of the fact that "catalectic," "consubstantial," and "costdrawer" are citizens in good standing of some large dictionary, that "contransmagnificandjewbangtantiality" is a molecule synthesized by him out of several such words, and that on a wholly different principle "lovelorn longlost lugubru Blooloohoom" is a comic coinage because it freezes in visual space some gesture of the tongue, the voice and the breath.

These auditory coinages deserve a bit of attention. Bloom's cat meows, and Joyce writes out the sound: "Mrkgnao!" Davy Byrne yawns, "Iiiiii-chaaaaaaach." The paperfolding machine speaks in its own way: "sllt." The fact that the dictionary gives no help to an author who wants to register phenomena of this kind attests to the

divorce between printing-case language, inhabiting technological space, and acoustic language, the intelligible creation of human speech. The ordinary words we speak inhabit both dimensions, and we shift from the visual to the
vocal manifestations of language with the negligence of
lifelong habit. But let an intelligible sound which the dictionary has omitted to register be transcribed according to
approved phonetic rules, and the result is taut, arbitrary
and grotesque: something living has been imperfectly synthesized out of those twenty-six interchangeable parts to
which every nuance of human discourse can allegedly be
reduced: as though technology were offering to reproduce
Helen of Troy with an Erector set. There is something
mechanical, Joyce never lets us forget, about all reductions
of speech to arrangements of twenty-six letters. We see him
playing in every possible way with the spatial organization
of printed marks: inserting headlines; reducing the themes
of an intricate Augustinian music to fifty-nine grotesque
permutable phrases, each printed at the head of the Sirens
episode on a separate line; entrusting the enervate languor
of Eumaeus to grey unbroken paragraphs that numb the
mind by tiring the eye; printing the questions and answers
of the great catechism with emphatic intervening spaces,
and the ultimate monologue of Mrs. Bloom with neither
paragraphs, commas nor full stops; and delivering what one
would expect to be the very epitome of the free and fluid, an
immense drunken phantasmagoria a fifth of the book in
length, into the keeping of the most rigid typographic for-
mality he employs anywhere: discrete speeches, capitalized
speakers, italicized narration: the status of everything visible at a glance.

What he thus freezes into a book is the life of Dublin,
chiefly its vocal life. Ireland, it is relevant and even com-

monplace to observe, is unique in the West for the exclusiveness of its emphasis on oral rather than typographic culture, and *Ulysses* is built about the antithesis between the personal matrix of human speech and the unyielding formalisms of the book as book. It can hardly be accidental that two Irishmen, Swift and Sterne,[6] exploited as long ago as the eighteenth century the peculiarities of the book to an extent no Anglo-Saxon has ever thought to emulate: nor is it accidental that the two of them link arms throughout *Finnegans Wake* like a pair of tutelary deities. Both of them were detached, as Joyce himself was later detached, from the assumptions of typographic culture: detached by the richer assumptions of a culture that thinks not of words but of voices, of the voice that states rather than the book that contains, of a matrix of speech in which person confronts person, not fact fact, of language generated by continuous acts of discourse rather than language delivered over to typographic storage. The Irish tradition of emitting pamphlets and broadsides rather than treatises, a tradition to which Joyce himself contributed in his youth, is an extension of these assumptions: the broadside is inalienably personal. It would be tempting to base a modern history of Ireland on the fact that the country has never sustained a large-scale publishing industry to erode its vocal and rhetorical bias, and polarize its sense of language toward the immutability of print rather than the coercive evanescence of breath. Even today it is customary for Dublin tavern wits to despise Joyce for practicing a lesser art than the talker's, a contempt sustained by something more than jealousy.

For nearly three centuries Ireland has mocked the book.

[6] I follow Joyce's usage, which makes Sterne an honorary Irishman. He was born in Ireland and spent much of his first ten years there.

Swift, we have seen, reached his most frenetic flights of ingenuity in the presence of the bookman's arsenal of techniques. Laurence Sterne availed himself of a hundred devices totally foreign to the storyteller but made possible by the book alone: not only the blank and marbled pages, the suppressed chapters represented only by headings, the blazonry of punctuation marks and the mimetic force of wavy lines, but also the suppression of narrative suspense—a suspense proper to the storyteller who holds us by curiosity concerning events unfolding in time—in favor of a bibliographic suspense which depends on our knowledge that the book in our hands is of a certain size and that the writer therefore has somehow reached the end of it—by what means? Nothing more completely separates typographic from oral narrative than the fact that, as we turn the pages, we can literally see the end coming. Following Swift and Sterne, Joyce shut a living world into a book, a heavy book that contains Dublin, kills it, and sets it into motion once again on a new plane: but a technological plane and a comic because finically precise motion. Dubliners tell discreditable stories about their enemies, and all Dublin knows the stories; but Joyce's revenge on Oliver Gogarty was to shut him into a book: a deed that crushed Gogarty more, despite the limited number of Dubliners who inspected the result, than any number of rumors: for in a book Buck Mulligan enacts the same formal ballet of irreverence, and emits the same delimited witticisms, for ever: always on schedule, always in the same context, always on the same pages: a precise definition of imaginative hell, ineluctable, unstoppable, unmodifiable. This preoccupation of Dublin wits with the book continues: both Flann O'Brien in *At Swim-Two-Birds* and Samuel Beckett in his great trilogy of French novels capitalize on the antisocial quality of literature, the fact that the writer is not speaking, is not drinking, is confronting nobody warming and warming to nobody, but exists shut away in a room setting on pieces of paper word after word which once they have passed through Gutenberg's machinery no afterthought will ever efface: a deed the very antithesis of everything that Irish culture prides itself on being.

IV

Joyce's techniques—it is one of his principal lessons—are without exception derived from his subject, often excerpted from his subject. They are not means of representing the subject, and imperfectly; they are the subject's very members laid on the page, in eloquent or ludicrous *collage*. His subject is Dublin, and a past Dublin, much of it alive in perishable memory, much of it already reduced to printed lists or shut away in printed books. Before *Ulysses* itself comes to an end, it must incorporate portions of a newspaper that was being printed while some of its events were being transacted. From this paper we learn that the remains of the late Mr. Patrick Dignam were interred at Glasnevin in the presence of, *inter alia*, "L. Boom"; like *Bouvard et Pécuchet* the book goes through the motions of picking up its own documentation. This particular document is a forgery, but what newspaper is not? *Ulysses* itself is certainly the forgery Joyce later called it in *Finnegans Wake*, joining in some ideal archive the hundreds of other printed documents June 16, 1904, has left behind. For Joyce was competing with his own materials, writing, as he was, in the midst of an economy of print, surrounded by other books on which to draw. He possessed, for example, Thom's Dublin Directory for the year 1904. He possessed the newspa-

Fig. 5 The young Joyce regarding his future hero

pers for the day he had chosen. He possessed dictionaries, in which to find the day's words and verify their spelling (it is worth remembering that Shakespeare had no dictionary). He possessed other books, in which he could find lists of all kinds: the colors of the Mass vestments, for example, and their significance. As days die, in the modern world, they pass into records, not merely, as did Homer's days, into memory. A certain day exists eternally at the point where the City Directory is intersected by the newspaper, the Gregorian and Liturgical calendars, the race results, the weather bureau statistics, the police blotter, and a million letters, diaries, cancelled checks, account books, betting tickets, laundry lists, birth certificates and cemetery registers.

Here we move beyond Flaubert; Flaubert, in quest of the general case, has none of Joyce's interest in lists. If many of Joyce's effects are the nearest English language equivalent to some of Flaubert's characteristic effects, yet even in brief examples one senses a pattern of difference, and the wider the range of examples the more marked the difference becomes. Consider, for instance, Joyce's concern with the arrangement of a limited number of words. He does this sentence by sentence and paragraph by paragraph (the Joycean paragraph deserves a chapter to itself; it is a unique creation), and by the time he has achieved the book we find it profitable, as Professor Hanley did, to regard the whole as a series of cunning permutations of some 30,000 different words. Or consider his collector's zeal. Frank Budgen once drew his attention to a word of Chatterton's and Joyce said, "It is a good word, and I shall probably use it": which he did. Or consider the care with which he stratifies the vocabulary of the various episodes, using in the lunchtime passage as many casual expressions derived from foodstuffs as he can collect, or in the funeral section a thousand mortuary turns of phrase. He appears to be working from lists, and for preference finite lists, beginning with the dictionary.

Discourse has become a finite list of words: at least potentially finite, since we can always imagine, without contradiction, a really complete dictionary, at least a really complete dictionary of the printed language. Dublin, 1904, in the same way has become the contents of Thom's Directory, in which it was possible for Joyce to verify in a moment the address of every business establishment, or the occupancy of every house (he was careful to install the Blooms at an address which, according to Thom's, was vacant). Theoretically, it would have been possible for him to name, somewhere in *Ulysses*, every person who inhabited Dublin on that day. Dublin, June 16, 1904, is documented in the newspapers of the day; Professor Richard Kain has shown with what care Joyce assimilated the names of the horses who were racing in the Gold Cup, or the details of the American steamboat disaster which occupied the Dublin headlines that morning. Even the nine participants in a quarter-mile footrace are embalmed forever in his text, name by name: M. C. Green, H. Thrift, T. M. Patey, C. Scaife, J. B. Jeffs, G. N. Morphy, F. Stevenson, C. Adderly and W. C. Huggard.

And we may note the congruence of such lists with other finite lists. There are twenty-four hours in a day, and he accounts for all but the ones spent by his characters in sleep. The spectrum has seven colors, and Bloom names them: roy g biv. The *Odyssey* can be dissociated into specific episodes, which Joyce accounts for. Shakespeare wrote some thirty-six plays; I do not know whether Joyce includes in the library scene an allusion to each of them, but it would not be surprising. The embryo lives nine months in the womb,

JAMES JOYCE: *Comedian of the Inventory*

or forty weeks; the body of the Oxen of the Sun episode has nine principal parts, in forty paragraphs, linked furthermore to a sequence of geological eras obtained from a list in a textbook.

We have heard of this side of Joyce often enough, but we have perhaps not heard the right things about it. As every commentator since Stuart Gilbert has discovered, nothing is easier than to disentangle, with patience, lists and more lists from the Protean text. What seems not to be dwelt upon is the fact that these lists are commonly finite, and that so far as he can, Joyce is at pains to include every item on them. What we can recover from his text is not a few samples, but the entire list. This is particularly clear in *Finnegans Wake*, where he had not, as in *Ulysses*, considerations of verisimilitude to impede him. Mr. James Atherton, in *The Books at the Wake*, has noted the presence in that work of all the titles of Shakespeare's plays, all of Moore's Irish Melodies, both the first line and the name of the tune, all the Books of the Bible, all the *suras* of the Koran (or not quite all; but whereas he speculates about the ones that are missing, it seems more likely that either he or Joyce simply overlooked them). Then there is the famous incorporation, into Anna Livia Plurabelle, of some six hundred rivers; probably not all the rivers of the world, but no doubt as many as Joyce could locate the names of. The same is true of the figures of rhetoric in the Aeolus episode of *Ulysses;* Mr. Gilbert, doubtless prompted by the author, cites ninety-four. I do not know whose enumeration Joyce followed, but I suspect he exhausted it, and if such a thing as an absolutely exhaustive list of figures of rhetoric were possible, and had been available to him, he would not have rested until he had accounted for every one.

This is the comedy of the Inventory, the comedy of exhaustion, comic precisely because exhaustive. The feeling proper to comic art, Joyce wrote, is joy, and by way of making clear what joy is, he distinguished it from desire. Now the virtue of exhaustiveness is this, that by it desire is utterly allayed. Nothing is missing. We have the double pleasure of knowing what should be present, and knowing that all of it is present. We have also what Bergson has taught us to regard as an indispensable component of the comic, a mechanical element; what is more mechanical than a checklist? And we have one other benison, an internal criterion of consistency. Celebrating a city, which once had walls and still has limits, which is laid out into streets and blocks, districts and zones, which can be represented by a map, or by a directory, Joyce is at pains to imitate all of these aspects of his subject in his book, which can be mapped and indexed, which has internal thoroughfares connecting points not textually contiguous, which contains zones defined and inimitably characterized (you could no more mistake a passage from "Eumaeus" for one from "Hades" than you could mistake Nighttown for Merrion Square).

V

It comes to us with renewed force, once we meditate on this analogy, how a city resembles a book, in having limits: in having limits, in being that which it is and not some other thing. *Integritas, consonantia, claritas:* Joyce's aesthetic speculations unite, with surprising aptness, the kind of art he proposed to practice, and the kind of subject that never left his mind.

He commences by quoting *pulcra sunt quae visa placent*, and explains that "sight" means "esthetic intellection," a mental process analogous with the process of vision. The difficulty in sustaining this analogy is obvious: sight is instantaneous, simultaneous, but works of literary art must be read through from beginning to end, in minutes or hours. In the stories of *Dubliners* he creates the illusion of a single static insight, like a painter's, by bringing everything to rest in a still tableau where all significance reposes. Eveline clutching the barrier, unable to go and unwilling to stay; Polly Mooney upstairs on her bed, barely able to distinguish between the "secret, amiable memories" of her intimacy with Mr. Doran and her mother's voice from below announcing that Mr. Doran has something to say to her; Gabriel Conroy gazing through a hotel bedroom window upon the falling snow. It is in a terminal scene of this kind that the purport of the narrative discloses itself. The narrative is quiet, circumstantial, owning no apparent direction. It is when we come to the terminal scene, which is what Joyce called the epiphany, that the pointless acquires sudden point, as though we were being shown a picture of which the narrative is preface and exegesis. This seems prompted by the "visa" of St. Thomas's formula; and two other orders of pictorial analogy may have operated in Joyce's mind. One of these is the fact that fiction, when he was young, was commonly accompanied by illustrations, whether in magazine or in book, and pictures, on the other hand, commonly implied stories. When Gabriel sees Gretta Conroy standing on the stairs listening to the hoarse voice of Mr. Bartell D'Arcy sing *The Lass of Aughrim* in the hall above, it at once occurs to him that if he were a painter he would paint her like that, and would call the picture "Distant Music." The pictures that went with published stories Joyce no doubt regarded as an impertinence—one can imagine what he would have said to any proposal to bring out *Dubliners* with illustrations—but they very likely helped suggest to him a mode of narrative art that would render the illustrator's services irrelevant, precisely by culminating in a scene possessing the repose, the sufficiency, the quiet plenitude, of an illustration. The other order of pictorial analogy that may have worked on his imagination is this, that the Epiphany itself is a favorite subject for painters.

Painting after painting shows, in the mean circumstances of a stable, many persons in repose: kings, shepherds, beasts, an infant and a mother, and everyone present has journeyed to this place, which confers meaning on their journeying, and brings them to a stability they have enjoyed, in the Christian imagination, for nearly twenty centuries. It is the longest, the most pervasive, the most intricate, static moment in the history of the West, and it seems to have suggested, to an Irish boy before whose imagination sermons and icons obtruded it for many years, the type of meaning to which the epiphanies of *Dubliners* aspire. We notice, for instance, that Joyce's people always journey to these revelations, and usually on foot. The principal activity in all his books is walking, walking the streets of Dublin, walking either to some goal or to some nemesis. A boy crosses the city at night, to Araby; and what is manifested to him at the end of his journey is an echoing and empty humiliation. An old woman crosses the city to a place of Halloween festivity; and what is manifested to her is an emblem of her death, a saucer of clay. Four friends bring their drunken companion the difficult journey to the place of salvation; and the epiphany that confronts them is blatant with shopkeepers' Christianity. *Dubliners* repeats and repeats this tale of the disappointed Magi, doubling the epiphany Joyce accords the reader with a counter-epiphany, an epiphany of absence, which mocks the travelers. Only in "The Boarding House," of all the fifteen stories, does no one come or go, everything transacted on premises to which the characters are steadily confined, but journey or no journey, the theme of empty revelation persists, as Bob Doran's intuitions of amatory bliss come to harsh fruition beneath the gaze of Mrs. Mooney. In the last story of all, Joyce seems to have imagined in Gabriel Conroy a disappointed St. Joseph, who discovers that his bride is already affianced to a ghost.

To pursue this theme is to discover anew how little room for maneuver Joyce's aesthetic intuitions accorded him. He commenced with two profound intuitions: that the Thomistic analogy with sight could guide the operations of a writer of prose fiction, that the analogy of the epiphany could govern the release of aesthetic clarity; and fifteen short stories employ very nearly the same mechanism of the empty epiphany, the disappointed journey with the tableau of frustration at the end of it. Not that the reader of *Dubliners* misses a more lively variety; the stories are true to their material, their insights, and their people; they revolve before us, with unforced compassion, a web of lives caught in the center of Irish paralysis. But the method is obviously not adapted to an extensive presentation of the city, the city that was Joyce's lifelong subject.

Now when he talks, or has Stephen talk, of *integritas, consonantia, claritas,* the talk is ostensibly of the aesthetic image; but the aesthetic image is already an abstraction considerably removed from the realities of a very long work in prose. We are free to suspect that in thinking of these things Joyce allowed his imagination to be steadied by the image not of his unwritten books but of their palpable subject, the city of Dublin; for it is manifestly true of a city that it is one thing, a thing of multiple interrelated parts, and that thing which it is; and that long experience will perhaps bring it whole into the imagination in an instant of radiant apprehension. There are no documents to prove that he was guided in this way by the analogies of the city; but if we allow ourselves to think so we can bridge the astonishing gap between *Dubliners* and *Ulysses*, and return to our earlier analogy between the city and the book. The physical book, first of all, one, whole, self-contained, bounded, in fact bound; populated with words; finite; delimited; bursting with self-contained activity and circular movement. And having determined, during some ten years' meditation, that he was going to write a book about a city, Joyce took stock, with the directness of genius, of the resources of the book as book: the physical bulk, the numbered pages, the facilities for endless cross-reference, the opportunities for visual display.

Now these are the precise aspects of the physical book which Encyclopaedias and Dictionaries exploit, but until *Ulysses*, novels (storybooks) had not thought to exploit them at all. The only advantage the physical format of the book confers on a novel like *Great Expectations* is portability and convenience of manufacture. There is no intrinsic reason why it should not be inscribed on an unrolling scroll, like the first scribal copies of *The Aeneid*. It is the books of reference that think to make use of leaves, sheets, numbered pages, and the fact that all pages of all copies are identical. The very sort of compilation which to Flaubert imaged the utter futility of the human spirit in its late phases, to Joyce represented an example and an opportunity. Consider the pains he takes to impede the motions of linear narrative; *Ulysses* is as discontinuous a work as its author can manage; we read it page by page, and once we have gotten the hang of it we can profitably read pages in isolation. We keep learning to pick up clues, and note them in the margin. We discover, from section to section, an increasing variousness of style, as though a committee of authors were at work. And we find, tucked into every available corner of the narrative, quantities of historical, cultural, civic, political and practical information, the sort of lore the Stoic exegetes were sure was secreted in Homer, here at last deliberately incorporated by the new chronicler of Ulysses's adventures, with the meticulousness our civilization has learned from its works of reference.

VI

Nothing is more important, for this sort of enterprise, than consistency of cross-reference. We are given, for instance, Bloom's, Stephen's and Molly's birth dates, and their ages on various past occasions are stated; so that when we are told that when Bloom was Stephen's present age Stephen was six, we can cross-check this information, to ascertain that it does indeed coincide with the time when Bloom and Molly met at Mat Dillon's. We may not check out many such references, but it is surprising how our sense of the book's integrity comes to depend on our faith that they will indeed check out. The past, in particular, is made to hang before us, an inflexible structure of incidence and coincidence, through which straight lines can be drawn. This sort of consistency was what Joyce came to understand by *consonantia,* the exact interrelation of parts; and apparently to value it, even to sense it, is a fairly late development of the Western imagination. Shakespeare notoriously doesn't bother to decide whether Lady Macbeth had any children or not. Shakespeare belonged to a predominantly oral tradition, and employed a predominantly auditory medium, in which the immediate effect is everything; but Joyce belongs

Fig. 6 Bloom reflected in John Ireland's window,
O'Connell Street

JAMES JOYCE: *Comedian of the Inventory*

to the age of the printed book, the numbered pages, and the cross-check. Joyce's readers belong to that age too, and he accords them, deliberately, its satisfactions.

We find him, then, in the generation after Flaubert, picking up Flaubert's fascination with the encyclopaedic and the meticulous, and deriving from it extraordinary and unsuspected values. It gave him a way of imaging the city; whereas it gave Flaubert merely a reason for despairing of humanity. And it gave his books a curious purity of concept, availing themselves of even the accidental features of the book itself, so that the printed book is no longer the record or depository of a story someone is conceived to be telling, nor as in Flaubert the scientific archive of an affair, but the essential artifact itself, declaring through its own inherent form the essential reality it means to show forth.

We have also, inherently, limitations. It was the very nature of Joyce's concept, that he should exhaust his material, or appear to exhaust it; he posits this theoretical possibility, in incorporating so many finite lists which he does exhaust. As we work our way through the latter part of the book we are likely to sense that we have encountered every ingredient before, and we come to suppose that there is only so much material, like the pieces of colored paper in a kaleidoscope, underlying all the brilliant configurations we see. The very letters of Bloom's name are permuted:

> Ellpodbomool
> Molldopeloob
> Bollopedoom
> Old Ollebo, M. P.

Having conceived *Ulysses* in such a way as to admit no random elements, since *integritas* and *consonantia* require that everything be necessary and interconnected, Joyce finds he must advert to as many things as possible at least twice, in order to demonstrate that nothing is a flyspeck on the design, but an intended part. In Eumaeus, in Ithaca, even in Penelope, the book, turned inward, takes inventory of itself. The last episode through which Bloom moves awake is a huge inventory of inventories: each of Bloom's books, each object on each shelf of the kitchen dresser, each piece of furniture in the parlor, each object in each of two locked sideboard drawers, each suspender button on Bloom's trousers (five; one missing), even each of the four occasions on which during the day the conjectured outcome of the Gold Cup race had been adverted to by others in his presence, or wrongly deduced by others from his behavior. And Bloom's ultimate ambition, the dream cottage with which he nightly solaces his imagination, takes shape through the book's most enormous inventory of all, whole catalogues emptied into the pages before us in a pointillist mercantile beatific vision. Causes are inventoried, effects are inventoried, principles are inventoried; even reasons for the disposition of obscure affections are supplied and then enumerated. Bloom's admiration of water, no doubt one of his least articulate passions, is amplified under forty-two separate and formal heads.

And out of so much inventory there grows a cyclical image of history, time's processes shuffling the same fifty-two cards for ever, in which it is difficult to distinguish the author's deepest convictions from the exigencies of his technique. True to his art, he takes stock of this sense of cycle and coincidence, which he cannot prevent our receiving from his methods, and puts it to use; it reproduces the tedium of the city, its continued identity in time, extricating similar civic patterns week after week, decade after decade, from a perpetually renewed supply of human lives (otherwise, how

JAMES JOYCE: *Comedian of the Inventory*

would Dublin in twenty years still be Dublin?) And it becomes a kind of prison, as for Joyce it was a kind of prison,
which he had neither escaped nor not escaped. It is an odd
fact, that the city which he loved above all other realities was
the sole reality to which it was forbidden to him to return.[7]

He put the closed form of his art to expressive use, then;
but it remains a closed form, which was Ezra Pound's reason for calling it a dead end. It is closed because it depends
on finite sets, that is to say on a branded and fettered past;
it deals only with retrospect. It is closed, furthermore, because in exploiting recurrence and coincidence, it succeeds
in suggesting the futility of all future art, since the elements
of all possible books will go into one book sufficiently comprehensive.

In his student days, Joyce tells us, he pondered "a garner
of slender sentences from Aristotle's Poetics and Psychology." Perhaps this garner contained bits of the *Metaphysics*
also, or perhaps he looked up the *Metaphysics* for himself.
Certainly he encountered, and meditated, the famous example of the man at the spring, for he paraphrases it in his
example of the girl who died in an accident to a hansom
cab, her heart pierced by a sliver of glass, and whose death,
he tells us, was not a tragic death. Aristotle's example concerns three intersecting chains of causality. One chain of
causality brings thirst to a man's throat, and impels him to
go to a little grove where there is a spring. A second brings
the spring to the surface of the ground at a certain spot, and

[7] Much has been made of the psychology of his exile; it bears noting that
his exile became final with the publication of *Dubliners*; for if after that
he had but set his right foot on Irish soil, he would have been detained
twenty years with lawsuits. Mr. Bartell D'Arcy himself, on first laying
eyes on "The Dead," went round at once to his solicitor; and Mr. Bartell D'Arcy was an old family friend, who had sung of a Saturday evening with Joyce's father. What of the host of indifferent or hostile people who discovered themselves in this book, or its successors?

sees to it that because of the moisture trees will grow up around it. A third brings brigands to the spot, and causes them to hide, as is reasonable, among the trees and hence by the spring. And the man coming to drink surprises them, and they kill him; and Aristotle holds that his death is wholly fortuitous.

It is fortuitous, although we can account for every step in the sequence of events that brought it about, because it is meaningless; three lines of causality intersect, and then go their ways; the man's death is an accident at their point of intersection. To raise the man's death to whatever intelligibility it admits, we commence to inventory the contributing facts. They reach far back in the past; they are perhaps infinitely numerous; we should ultimately find ourselves explaining why he was born in this part of the world, instead of in Zanzibar, and so going into the fortunes of his ancestors, and doing the same service for each of his assailants; and we should never stop. If we choose to tell the story of his death, we make an arbitrary beginning; and part of Joyce's point, in modeling on this example of Aristotle's the example he uses in his aesthetic argument, is precisely that any beginning would be arbitrary. Chains of causality reach back in time forever.

All Joyce's instincts, as he meditated facts of this kind— facts that confront anyone who proposes to write a novel and wonders where to begin it—predisposed him to seek chains that were not infinite, which could only mean that they were circular. So in a thousand ingenious ways he makes it seem that his infinite material is inherently self-contained. This the city makes plausible, imposing boundaries; and he causes Bloom to have been acquainted with Mrs. Riordan, who lived for a few years in the Dedalus household (she is the "Dante" of the *Portrait*), and brings

JAMES JOYCE: *Comedian of the Inventory*

Stephen Dedalus, aged six to the notice of Leopold Bloom
and Marion Tweedy at a time when Leopold Bloom is the
age Stephen is to be when their paths cross again; and again
when Stephen is as old as Bloom's dead son would be today
were he alive. Or he gives Molly a tale of previous lovers,
enumerated very late in the book, and plants most of their
names at some point earlier in the text. As we confront such
instances we receive the impression that whatever line we
follow into the past of this book, it will meet some other line
equally traceable, and return upon itself; we receive, that is,
once again the impression of a finite set of materials, finite
in reality as they must be finite in the book, of which the
book is the adequate exemplar. Our ultimate sense of the
book, or one mode of our ultimate sense of it, is this: that
it is the minute and reliable and exhaustive inventory of all
the facts that it incorporates, or even implies. On this is
based the endlessly diverting joy of recognizing what we
have seen before, of noting that when Philip Drunk and
Philip Sober appear in the Circe hallucination pushing lawn-
mowers "purring with a rigadoon of grasshalms" (508),
they double with a deaf gardener on page 9, outside the window where an Oxford rag is in progress, who "pushes his
mower on the sombre lawn watching narrowly the dancing
motes of grasshalms." Even the odd word "grasshalms" re-
curs. This is the comedy of inventory, the comedy of the
closed system, in which we constantly recognize known
things in new fantastic guises; and it is the dead end which
Joyce triumphantly prosecuted until it became exactly the
image of the city he loved for its variety and distrusted for
its poverty of resource.

3. Samuel Beckett:

COMEDIAN OF THE IMPASSE

I

LET US BEGIN by assuming Samuel Beckett's existence. More than one traveler has returned with tales of spending a few hours in Paris with a man who claimed to be he. But anyone can make claims. Certainty would entail seeing this man writing a book, and furthermore a book later published with Samuel Beckett's name on it. And certainty would still be less than absolute; one might feel in need of proof that he was actually composing the book in question, and not simply writing it down from memory. This note of uncertainty plagues the whole Beckett cosmos, where the reliability of a witness is always open to question. For the very existence of the celebrated Godot we have really only the word of two boys, whose testimony is in other respects less than satisfactory; and if dubiety of this order can infect a play, where we can see many things for ourselves, we should expect the reliability of the fiction to be still lower. Nothing confronts our senses but a set of printed words, assembled by we cannot say whom with we cannot tell what authority; and not only is the work of uncertain credit, but it can also entoil us in whatever doubts are felt, or allegedly felt, by the man who is writing, or says he is.

SAMUEL BECKETT: *Comedian of the Impasse*

Thus Beckett's 1961 novel, *Comment C'est*, terminates amid utter despair as to the possibility of deciding whether the preceding 180 pages have told us anything reliable or not; the narrator's only terminal certainty is that it is totally dark and that he is lying face down in the only element there is, which is mud. He is not even clear how it is that he has arranged to get a written record into our hands. He is inclined to postulate a certain Krim who writes down his babblings and ascends with them into the light, but this is a hypothesis and uncertain, like all hypotheses. It is not really certain that there is any light for Krim (if he exists) to ascend to, though there appear to be memories (if they are memories) of a sojourn amid visible things, once, long ago (if expressions of time have any meaning). His own name he does not divulge; presumably he has none; and while other beings in the course of the narrative are equipped with identifying sounds, all very similar (Bim, Bom, Pim, Krim, Kram, Pam Prim), it seems clear that these are not really their names (whatever that means) but simply convenient ways of referring to them (if they exist).

One could make out a strong case for the narrator's name being Sam, but it is not clear what such a statement would mean. For how can a character in fiction be said to have a real name, if the author does not tell us what it is? There exists a letter signed "Sam. Beckett" which compounds these difficulties by carefully referring to the figure in question as "the narrator/narrated," which apparently means that if he, the character, is inventing the book then someone else is inventing him; and perhaps it is the name of the someone else that is supposed to be Sam.

This is, on the whole, the way things generally are, *in terra Samuelis*. Clearly we are at the farthest possible remove from the omniscient narrator who has so much of our fiction in his trust. That omniscient narrator has always created a certain embarrassment, not mitigated by talk about "point of view." Novelists have been at endless logical shifts to explain how he came by his information. He discovered a bundle of documents; he happened to be nearby and saw it all; he heard the story from someone at his club; Thackeray, more honest than most, denominated him "puppet-master" and told the truth, which was that he knew the whole story because he made it all up. Beckett, on the whole, takes Thackeray's hint; it is, indeed, all made up, and gripping as it is, we aren't to rely on it. Alas, the man who makes it up is made up too, may even be making himself up. A figure called Moran commences his half of the novel *Molloy* by writing: "It is midnight. The rain is beating on the windows. I am calm. All is sleeping. Nevertheless I get up and go to my desk. . . . My name is Moran, Jacques. That is the name I am known by. I am done for. . . ." He proceeds to tell us, in 38,000 clear and simple words, the narrative of how he came to be done for, how he went on a journey and how he came back home stripped, discredited, ruined. The narrative ends, "Then I went back into the house and wrote, It is midnight. The rain is beating on the windows. It was not midnight. It was not raining."

This is, quite explicitly, the paradox of the Cretan liar: all Cretans are liars, said the man from Crete. It has always been inherent in the novel, the supposed narrator of which is part of the narration. That a puzzle out of the logic classrooms should confront us at the threshold of this familiar and straightforward form should occasion no surprise; the novel has always been deeply involved with logic, more so than any other genre. That is why generations of novelists, who seem to the casual eye only folk with a tale to tell, have twisted and turned in attempting to justify logically the very

SAMUEL BECKETT: *Comedian of the Impasse*

convention under which they are operating, the convention of somebody knowing the inner recesses of a tale so intimately. This sort of problem troubles no other literary practitioner; Homer, in fact, exorcises it by appealing to the Muse, and it was customary to do likewise, or else to appeal to an older book (such as Homer's), until the novel was invented. But a novel declines to be a Muse's song, or even a man's invention; it aspires, or feigns to aspire, to the truth of history, of scientific history. It is the bastard child begotten by empirical science upon a dormant Muse, and it has been cursed with logical crosses from the day it learned to talk.

Beckett took it up at the point to which James Joyce had brought it. There is a kind of symbolic justice in his long personal intimacy with Joyce, and in the fact that both of them preferred to conduct their operations in Flaubert's capital. For Beckett is the heir of Joyce as Joyce is the heir of Flaubert, each Irishman having perceived a new beginning in the impasse to which his predecessor seemed to have brought the form of fiction; and Beckett in particular, by an act of imaginative superfoetation, sought to solve the general problem, how to deal with an impasse. He is the comedian of the impasse, as Joyce of the inventory and Flaubert of the encyclopaedia.

And we have been tracing the route to an impasse. We have seen Flaubert confronting fiction's gargantuan appetite for fact, for detail, for documentation, and discerning that it is the one form of literary art that traffics in empirical certainties. The unit of its prose is not the word, but the statement. Its art is the art of the declarative sentence: It is midnight. The rain is beating on the windows. But as the declarative sentences people exchange when they talk are mostly half-truths, or untruths, so the novels they read are mostly romances, half-baked and illusory, the sort of reading matter that destroyed Emma Bovary's sense of fact. Flaubert regarded ideal fiction as aspiring to a scientific order of general truth, arrived at, on the model of that Stoic of the intellect, the nineteenth-century scientist, by a rigorous process of observation and scrutiny. But what lay before him to observe was human gullibility, human willingness to exchange cliches, in short human stupidity, of the kind that is willing to listen to the Encyclopaedia salesman. If that is the novelist's material, the only material there is, then the Flaubertian novel must arrive, by a more laborious route (we have seen how), at a trajectory parallel to that executed by the hack. The hack draws his freehand curves; the Flaubertian novelist performs a laborious, critical reconstruction of these arcs, with infinite care and calculation. They still mean little, but they mean it meaningfully. Hence *Madame Bovary* is from beginning to end the knowing rescription of a shilling romance of adultery, critically and scrupulously examining the material to which the latter is faithful by a kind of inner light. And the Flaubertian novel, furthermore, if it observes people being stupid and superficial, examines, embalms, their stupidities and superficialities. It finds itself, at last, turned into a scientific instrument, of encyclopaedic scope, an encyclopaedia of the null; and at last it concerns itself with two men seeking to engorge all knowledge. The two men, in turn, were to write the second half of the novel. Compiling in the twilight of their grand illusion a classified encyclopaedia every line of which Flaubert had found for them in other books, they were to grow at last—how could they help it?—indistinguishable from their author, who had himself pursued every detail of their imbecile researches into books where (he knew in advance, as they did not) nothing was to be found.

SAMUEL BECKETT: *Comedian of the Impasse*

And were they great lunatics, or was he? For them at least
hope had always been alive, but Flaubert labored years on
end through systems of agriculture, aesthetics, mnemonotechnic, in the steady cold certainty that he was wasting his
labor.

At this point Joyce makes a new start. He takes over
from Flaubert two great principles: (1) that the novel has
an encyclopaedic capacity for fact; (2) that the novel can
most fruitfully approach its social material by parody. He
did not, however, share the Frenchman's famous ecstasy of
disgust. Though he mocked Dublin he loved it as he loved
nothing else.

Thus he does not adopt, as Flaubert does, the ideal role
of severe detachment. He can play at detachment, as he can
play at everything else; but it is for him only one gambit
among twenty. Flaubert would have been stayed by the
rules he had adopted, no less than by temperament, from
writing anything like the Cyclops episode in *Ulysses* ("So we
turned into Barney Kiernan's and there sure enough was the
citizen up in the corner having a great confab with himself
and that bloody mangy mongrel, Garryowen, and he wait-
ing for what the sky would drop in the way of drink")—
reproducing for fifty pages the Dublin argot not only with
scientific precision but with admiration and joy. Writing
such books is not unlike playing an intricate game. Joyce's
temperament, and his material, are accommodated by a different set of rules. What he does, by way of incorporating
his material, is enumerate and inventory its riches. But
again logic closes in. The delights of enumeration lead him
inexorably to another principle, the book as a closed system,
containing, even replacing, all that it concerns itself with;
since the very notion of the inventory implies that the set of
things inventoried is complete. The spirit, as with Flaubert,

is still scientific; but the method is now to master the material by exhausting it; and then permute it and exhibit it and reexhibit it until every relevant category is filled and fulfilled, and all Dublin and all knowledge grow coterminous.

And not only all Dublin and all knowledge: all Dublin and this book. For implying as it does the exhaustive application of Gutenberg technology, *Ulysses* approximates, or clearly suggests that it is approximating, to its own Platonic idea, the book as book, of which familiar books are but special cases. The more it exploits the devices of permutation which print suggests, the more it implies that the limits of permutation are its real binding form.

Joyce went on, of course, to *Finnegans Wake,* a book that even more than *Ulysses* is inconceivable without the mediation of print and the endless inventorying print impies. Print is the very *form* of this last work. It is print that fixes and defines the fluid metamorphoses of all the voices in Europe, constantly tugging the vocal into the magnetic field of alphabetical, permuting vowels according to plan, alpha and omega, a, e, i, o, u: coolly insisting on the power of just twenty-six letters over all of speech, and according each deliquescent dream-coinage the delimitation, the *status,* of a printed word. This book of words that are not words employs to a still greater extent than *Ulysses* those discontinuities first explored by Swift: discontinuities which the format of the book itself will serve to unify.

Passage is juxtaposed with passage, phrase with phrase, not in the economy of speech but on the page. And still more than *Ulysses* it dispenses with narrative in time. Time-ridden according to its own proclamation, time-obsessed because it distills voices that search forward in time, it yet

SAMUEL BECKETT: *Comedian of the Impasse*

inhabits typographic space, drawing not towards some narrative finale but towards its own last page, the page next to its back cover, and then circling forward to do the only thing the reader can do who has reached the end of a book and has no other book: begin again.

Nothing is more characteristic of the book as book than its obliviousness to chronological pressure. Time is not its currency, time is what the reader brings to it ("the ideal reader suffering from an ideal insomnia"). The book is a spatial phenomenon, an affair of pages that turn when we please to turn them, incorporating no hurry, no impatience. In technological space the word, as we have seen, is self-sufficient; so in the ultimate book are paragraphs, chapters, sections: *Ulysses* has eighteen and *Finnegans Wake,* seventeen, succeeding one another with economy and necessity but no urgency, like Pound's *Cantos,* the sections of *The Waste Land* (a poem with numbered lines and footnotes), or the static effects in Wyndham Lewis's *Childermass.* In an expansive quiet which has led some writers to consider oriental analogies, the book as book deploys its blocks of print, incorporating all that the writer knows, or all (it tries to convince us) that mankind has thought or said, in its soothing unhurried arrangements and rearrangements of twenty-six bits of type.

And here is another impasse. First Flaubert, then Joyce, pursuing to the end a set of rigorous principles, arrives each of them at a work that seems, in the abstract, barely worth the doing, and that once done seems to leave little to do. The result, in every case, is a piece of virtuosity upon which it does not seem possible to improve. Enter, to this impasse, Samuel Beckett.

II

Beckett's first strategy is a strategy of survival. If it is impossible to carry competence further, he will see what can be done with incompetence. And plucking the fruits of incompetence—plays that seem unable to get the title character onto the stage, novels that issue merely in the fact that someone is sitting in bed writing a novel, or that founder amid logical perplexities of their own propounding —he evolves meanwhile, since his mind is never still, a yet more comprehensive theory of what the writer is doing with himself, and a yet more general set of rules for the game he plays. (We should mock art if we pretended that it was something less than a game. Any Frenchman can be a French bum. Anyone at all can write *reportage* about bums, French or other. Only genius, and Irish genius for choice, can play with finesse the dark game of *pretending to be* a French bum.)

In a series of three short dialogues on painting, Beckett, with the assistance of the Frenchman Georges Duthuit, makes his only, but sufficient, general statement on the role of incompetence in the arts. The first dialogue establishes the not unreasonable principle that competence, however great, always fails. We invariably see aspects in which the work falls short. Competence, furthermore, regards the world always from the same point of view, as a challenge to its resources, a challenge it can never wholly meet. So art as it evolves moves step by step "along the dreary road of the possible," always looking for something that can be done, and then seeking means to do it, and never quite succeeding. The second phase of this argument follows from the first: we can easily imagine a painter who notes that the common element in all art is partial failure, and determines to take as his theme paint's incapacity to rival reality. But here we have simply another form of competence: "No painting is more replete than Mondrian's." In the presence of art however abstract, however self-denying, we have still, as Beckett phrases it, two familiar maladies: "the malady of wanting to know what to do and the malady of wanting to be able to do it." Even emptiness becomes something to be possessed. So the dialogue moves to its third phase, in which Beckett advances the notion of utter and uncalculating incapacity, producing an art which is "bereft of occasion in every shape and form, ideal as well as material."

> The situation is that of him who is helpless, cannot act, in the end cannot paint, since he is obliged to paint. The act is of him, who, helpless, unable to act, acts, in the event paints, since he is obliged to paint.
> —Why is he obliged to paint?
> —I don't know.
> —Why is he helpless to paint?
> —Because there is nothing to paint and nothing to paint with.

If for "paint" we substitute "write," we have exactly the situation of the man in *Comment C'est*. There is nothing to write, nothing to write with; it is totally dark; nothing comes to the ears but his own voice, nothing to the nose, fingers or tongue but universal mud. And he achieves an eloquent book, in Archimedean equilibrium, 180 pages long, in three equal parts, beautifully and tightly wrought.

Art is the perfect not-doing of what cannot be done, and peer as we will, we shall not discern Beckett *doing*. We are encumbered by no proof sheets, no keys, no outlines. There is no legend of the fabulous artificer. Not even the

Paris telephone directory records his presence, though it did Joyce's. Photographs display the somewhat bemused expression of a man to whom numerous books have mysteriously happened. We do not track theme-words through the text of *Comment C'est* or *Happy Days,* marveling at the master's virtuosity. On the contrary, we note the stubborn (though fastidious) repetitiousness of a man who can barely keep going ("end at last of the second part how it was with Pim now only the third and last how it was after Pim before Bom how it is there is how it was with Pim"). His role is not the engineer's but the scribe's, or the medium's ("I say it as I hear it"). Any hack could instruct him in the elements of his craft, though it is not clear whether he would profit by instruction, for his virtuosity, such as it is, appears to diminish rather than grow accomplished. The early *Murphy* is at least something like a novel. It has even a timetable, and one would have expected practice to increase its author's facility. Five novels later, alas, he seems unable to punctuate a sentence, let alone construct one. More and more deeply he penetrates the heart of utter incompetence, where the simplest pieces, the merest three-word sentences, fly apart in his hands. He is the non-maestro, the anti-virtuoso, habitue of nonform and anti-matter, Euclid of the dark zone where all signs are negative, the comedian of utter disaster.

The road to this ideal incapacity is long and intricate. Beckett's first step, in the mature phase of his career which began in France during the war, was to commence where *Ulysses* left off, with the comedy of the inventory. He does this in *Watt,* his last novel in English, and *Watt's* point of departure is the Ithaca episode of *Ulysses.* In the Ithaca episode Joyce produces the great scientific catechism, in which all the empirical data of the book get revolved before the reader "in the barest and coldest way." It is a particularly sensitive spot in the tissue of *Ulysses*, since it is the point of growth where Joyce explicitly tackles and develops the encyclopaedism of Flaubert, which Flaubert had brought to a dead end. Here is what the catechism tells us about Bloom's entry into the house:

> Resting his feet on the dwarf wall, he climbed over the area railings, compressed his hat on his head, grasped two points at the lower union of rails and stiles, lowered his body gradually by its length of five feet nine inches and a half to within two feet ten inches of the area pavement, and allowed his body to move freely in space by separating himself from the railings and crouching in preparation for the impact of the fall.

For this passage Joyce is known to have undertaken special research; he despatched his Aunt Josephine to Number 7 Eccles Street to verify whether a man of medium height would be capable of negotiating this leap without injury. So fiction (Bloom's size) becomes fact, and fact (the areaway at 7 Eccles St.) is incorporated into fiction, and both meet in the inventory of facts, two more items in the encyclopaedia of Dublin. Now here is Beckett:

> Watt's way of advancing due east, for example, was to turn his bust as far as possible towards the north and at the same time to fling out his right leg as far as possible towards the south, and then to turn his bust as far as possible towards the south and at the same time to fling out his left leg as far as possible towards the north, and then again to turn his bust as far as possible towards the north and to fling out his right leg as far as possible towards the south, and then again to turn his bust as far as possible towards the south and to fling out his left leg as far as possible towards the north, and so on, over and over again, many many times, until he

Fig. 7 Watt walking

SAMUEL BECKETT: *Comedian of the Impasse*

reached his destination, and could sit down. So, standing first on one leg, and then on the other, he moved forward, a headlong tardigrade, in a straight line. The knees, on these occasions, did not bend. They could have, but they did not. No knees could better bend than Watt's, when they chose, there was nothing the matter with Watt's knees, as may appear. But when out walking they did not bend, for some obscure reason. Notwithstanding this, the feet fell, heel and sole together, flat upon the ground, and left it, for the air's uncharted ways, with manifest repugnancy. The arms were content to dangle, in perfect equipendency.

If this, in the abstractness of its language and the gravity of its cadence, evidently resembles the Ithaca section of *Ulysses,* it differs still more markedly. It is more general; it tells us about Watt's way of advancing due east, for example, not of how Watt went to a particular place; there is nothing for an Aunt Josephine to go and verify. Yet strangely enough it is at the same time more particular, since Bloom jumps as any man would have jumped, but Watt's way of advancing due east, for example, is so far as we can tell peculiar to Watt. It is as though Watt were the legitimate object of sober curiosity, scientific observation, and minute recording, in order to augment mankind's small stock of reliable knowledge. And we note too a certain mimetic fullness, for not one complete pair of steps is fully described, but two, to make sure they are alike, before the generalization is risked that all the others are similar, until Watt gets to his destination, and can sit down. But here another force is frankly at play, namely the writer's pen setting down words, and then setting down more words, and then setting down the same words over again, so that we have before us a piece of writing, and a piece of writing with little of great importance to communicate, indeed a fiction which is at the same time an exercise in symmetry and ritual.

The more we read of *Watt,* indeed, the more does the grave determination to recover and record all that is knowable of this eerie character compromise and contradict itself; for more and more palpably the book is a composition, ritualistic, repetitious, compulsive: and the detached, encyclopaedic style more and more evidently rehearses not facts but possibilities, not evidences but speculation. Thus for half a page we pursue the minutiae of Watt's indecision, whether to shut the door, from which he feels a draught, and set down his bags, and sit down, or to shut the door, and set down his bags, without sitting down, or to shut the door, and sit down, without setting down his bags, and so on, for eight possibilities, including the possibility of leaving things as they are. A technique of inventory very like Joyce's is handling less and less real material; and the closed system indispensable to inventory is no longer, as it tended to become for Joyce, the closed system of the transacted past, but the closed system of possibilities arrived at, amid given presupposed data, by logical analysis. And logical analysis pertains to a mental world; what Beckett is doing is subtracting from the methods of *Ulysses* all the irreducible realities of Joyce's Dublin, and so transposing the novel to a plane of empty but oddly gripping construction.

Already in *Watt* we notice our author's paradoxical fecundity. A five-man examining committee exchanges glances; and the narrative of their mutual interrogation commences. "They then began to look at one another, and much time passed, before they succeeded in doing so. Not that they looked at one another long, no, they had more sense than that. But when five men look at one

SAMUEL BECKETT: *Comedian of the Impasse*

another, though in theory only twenty looks are necessary, every man looking four times, yet in practice this number is seldom sufficient, on account of the multitude of looks that go astray. For example . . ." More than three pages later the inventory of looks is still going on, and "of the five times eight, or forty looks taken, not one has been reciprocated, and the committee, for all its twisting and turning, is no further advanced, in this matter of looking at itself, than at the now irrevocable moment of its setting out to do so. And this is not all." Indeed it is not all; and two more closely printed pages are to elapse before the question of five men exchanging glances has been laid to rest, and a suitable method for accomplishing this outlined. The policy of the book appears to be this, that the more trivial the matter the more space is devoted to its analysis. Nor is this sheer perversity; for the more trivial the matter the more completely do all its particular data lie within the writer's control, to be arranged, enumerated, commented on, exhausted, whereas a matter of some moment—like the death of Aristotle's thirsty man—entails so many factors, so many intersecting chains of causality, so many possibilities realized, not realized, or not even recognized, that art quails before it and is content with a perfunctory sentence. For instance, in the second part of *Molloy:*

> He thrust his hand at me. I have an idea I told him once again to get out of my way. I can still see the hand coming towards me, pallid, opening and closing. As if self-propelled. I do not know what happened then. But a little later, perhaps a long time later, I found him stretched on the ground, his head in a pulp. I am sorry I cannot indicate more clearly how this result was obtained, it would have been something worth reading.

A page later, however, he has no difficulty supplying 300 words on the steps by which he gathered up his keys, which had been scattered on the ground. It seems obvious that this narrator can tell us everything except what we usually count on narrators to tell us in stories. This is one thing Beckett means by exploiting incompetence.

Another thing he means by exploiting incompetence is this: that the novel can be released from the impasse of virtuosity if it is sufficiently, literally, even idiotically faithful to its own nature. And its own nature is to be (who can doubt it?) a sheaf of papers filled by a man alone in a room, writing.

An Irish tradition at least as old as *A Tale of a Tub* has generated books by men whose theme is that they are writing books. The pretended author of *A Tale of a Tub* is pluming himself mightily on the fact that he is going to extract money from the booksellers although he has nothing to say. Beckett, however, is not toying with the reader at all. He presumably has no reader. His sham-authors are very diligently writing as best they can, either like the dying Malone to pass the time, or else like The Unnamable because by writing they may be at last released from the obligation to write. They are doing their very best, and it is not much, to make as clear as possible what little they know; for as every handbook informs us, the novelist writes about what he knows. Malone writes two pages on the coat worn by his character Macmann, concluding with half a page on the buttons; and who will know the coat of Macmann, and the buttons on it, if not Macmann's creator? Here is his account:

> Now with regard to the buttons of this coat, they are not so much genuine buttons as little wooden cylinders two or three inches long, with a hole in the middle for the thread, for one

hole is ample, though two and even four are more usual, and this because of the inordinate distension of the buttonholes consequent on wear and tear. And cylinders is perhaps an exaggeration, for if some of these little sticks or pegs are in fact cylindrical, still more have no definable form. But all are roughly two and a half inches long, and thus prevent the lappets from flying apart, all have these features in common. Now with regard to the material of this coat, all that can be said is that it looks like felt. And the various dints and bulges inflicted upon it by the spasms and contortions of the body subsist long after the fit is past. So much for the coat. I'll tell myself stories about the boots another time, if I can.

This is careful, grave, finical, responsible; Flaubert himself was not more scrupulous of fact. Indeed Malone makes the great novelists of the past look like paraphrasers. He communicates the great pleasure only exactness can give, the pleasure of knowing, like an observant child, exactly how several makeshift buttons are shaped, and how the thread passes through them, and the pleasure, for which the child is not yet equipped, of placing this knowledge in a perspective of maturer knowledges, of reason, cause, effect and function. And this pleasure is his because he is simply amusing himself, he is not preparing an effect or sketching an atmosphere or anticipating with cunning strokes a climax. It is a great relief, when fiction has gotten so knowing, to be free of such expertise, for a while.

Yet in extracting all these virtues from the impasse, the impasse of having nothing much to say and no reason for saying it, Beckett succeeds in not at all wasting our time. For since someone else, a character, is responsible for the narration, we are not simply considering buttons, but attending to the intimate deliverances of a human mind, which in finding the buttons of absorbing interest, proves to be itself of absorbing interest, to us. That is what is misleading about quotations from Beckett's novels. The quotations are likely to be about buttons, or stones, or even a photograph of a donkey wearing a straw hat, or else about problems, and those problems of little intrinsic import. But the context from which they are excerpted is one of intimate human concern; these topics, these questions, have all occurred to a mind, indeed as we encounter them are in the immediate act of occurring to a mind, which appeals to us by its very proximity. So true is this, that it soon becomes meaningless to say that the presence of this fictive person, and his interest, redeems topics of no intrinsic interest; for how can a question have no intrinsic interest, when someone is so passionately interested in it? And we learn to grow as intensely concerned as Molloy, when he struggles for eight pages to devise a system for sucking systematically, without gap or duplication, on each of sixteen stones, over and over, when he has only four pockets in which to keep track of them. No doubt a similar itch for symmetry tormented the great Newton, to whom we have all learned to say that we are deeply indebted.

And we are back, oddly enough, where Flaubert left us, in the presence of a man doggedly performing research; but not research into the idiotic opinions in books, but research into the logical foundations of the universe, which cleverer people have perhaps vanquished, but which he must have the experience of assaulting for himself; for there are intellectual experiences so simple and fundamental that it is not possible to inherit them. And non-intellectual experiences too. Malone must die for himself, unaided.

This fiction differs from Flaubert's and Joyce's in another way: though no detail is too minute for its attention, its world is cleared, to an unprecedented degree, of impedimenta. The characters possess next to nothing, and the world around them, furthermore, contains very little: a tree or two, or four walls and a window. Malone must even consider in some detail how he shall distinguish, in the room to which he is confined, his possessions from his non-possessions; for since he is bedridden there can be no question of use, and since he is always alone, no criterion that sets *meum* off from *tuum*. The Beckett characters wear greatcoats and hats, and they generally take the precaution of securing the hat beneath the chin, with a string. Malone has even removed the brim from his, so he can keep it on in bed. Bouvard and Pécuchet were making a fathomless act of faith in human receptivity to information, when they supposed that their hats would remain their own if they simply inscribed their names inside. Greatcoats and hats, then, and boots, or in Watt's case a boot and a shoe; and the memories of what must have once been a substantial education. They are always being surprised at the oddments of fact they remember; but what sticks mainly is a clear sense of declarative syntax, a chaste but adequate vocabulary, and a fondness for calculations. And these, plus a few objects, such as stones, carrots, a bicycle or two, a piece of string, are the ingredients with which Beckett's fictional enterprise operates.

III

It is easy to say that he has reached a dead end; the fact remains that he, at any rate, has not. He can discard piece after piece, and still hold our attention with a new book. In *Comment C'est*, he reduces the *mise-en-scène* to mud, total darkness, a cord, a can opener, and a jute sack filled with tinned fish. He even does without the sentence. And the amazing thing about *Comment C'est* is the way these simple objects proliferate. In obedience to purely logical laws, by the time the book is two-thirds over, the empty world is filled with an infinite number of beings, with social rituals, with memories, with educational processes and private lives, with mountains of tinned fish, millions of sacks, and even scribes, whole hierarchies of scribes. There is not a flaw in the process by which all this is generated; it fills the recumbent narrator with consternation, and he is reduced to waving it all away as illusion. Novels of course are characteristically replete, stuffed with facts and objects, but seldom at the obedience of inner laws so compulsive.

Where do the thousands on thousands of things come from, that clutter *Ulysses*? From a convention. "His hand took his hat from the peg over his initialled heavy overcoat. . . ." Four nouns, and the book's world is heavier by four things. One, the hat, "Plasto's high grade," will remain in play to the end. The hand we shall continue to take for granted: it is Bloom's; it goes with his body, which we are not to stop imagining. The peg and the overcoat will fade. "On the doorstep he felt in his hip pocket for the latchkey. Not there. In the trousers I left off." Four more things. "He pulled the halldoor to after him very quietly, more, till the footleaf dropped gently over the threshold, a limp lid." Three things more. "He crossed to the bright side, avoiding the loose cellarflap of number seventyfive. The sun was nearing the steeple of George's church." Yet more things. It is clear that Joyce has chosen a convention which exacts the continuous creation of the environment through which Bloom moves, so that to get Bloom out of the house he must be supplied, in rapid succession, with a hat to put on, a peg from which to take it, a door to open and shut, a key to feel for and a hip pocket in which not to find it, absent trousers in which to have left it, a street to step into, a sun to light the street: each of these things summoned into fictive being as it is needed. By the time such a character has gotten to the end of the street the list of properties would cover sheets of foolscap. By the time he has concluded the action of a novel which requires him to walk around town all day, sheer *things* are growing innumerable, wedging into the very dialogue—

> (. . . *A cake of new clean lemon soap arises, diffusing light and perfume.*)

> THE SOAP
> We're a capital couple are Bloom and I;
> He brightens the earth, I polish the sky.

or simulating, in illimitable cascade, an advertisement canvasser's beatific vision:

> . . . fumed oak sectional bookcases containing the Encyclopaedia Britannica and New Century Dictionary, transverse obsolete mediaeval and oriental weapons, dinner gong, alabaster lamp, bowl pendant, vulcanite automatic telephone receiver with adjacent directory, . . . bentwood perch with a fingertame parrot (expurgated language), . . . water closet on mezzanine provided with opaque singlepane oblong window, tipup seat, bracket lamp, brass tierod brace, armrests, footstool and artistic oleograph on inner face of door. . . .

These things get onto the page, and there take up our time, because the writer is at pains to name them, and write down their names, deliberately and successively. A book is a construction of words which we encounter one after another. A cine camera trained on the moving Bloom would blot up every instant a hundred objects which would exert no claim on our attention whatever: which would never be lingered on, never even be named. In a photograph a cat has whiskers because it has. In a book it is supplied with whiskers, named and explicit whiskers, so that Bloom can speculate: "Wonder is it true if you clip them they can't mouse after. Why? They shine in the dark perhaps, the tips. Or kind of feelers in the dark, perhaps." The things, so many named things, are cues for Bloom's mental processes, which constitute the book's real business. And this is a convention, to be distinguished with care from the practice of quotidian novelists who dust their pages lightly with detail—"She turned away. Through the leaded panes sunlight poured onto a dusty piano."—to impart a random feel of reality. This convention is traceable as far back as Flaubert, who was at pains to supply objects—a Jesuit, a wedding party, a drunken workman—for Bouvard and his new friend Pécuchet to converse about, and who at intervals during so many years collected and alphabetized so many objects—PYRAMIDE; BACCALAURÉAT; ARCHIMEDE[1]; ÉPOQUE (LA NÔTRE)—together with the bits of conversation they can be counted on to elicit. And it is traceable further back still, to Jonathan Swift, who installed his fictional hero Lemuel Gulliver in the center of a universe of objects, to whose sizes, weights, measurements, surfaces, smells, he is infallibly responsive.

Swift, constructing a satire on mindless empiricism, achieved a Flaubertian novel twelve decades ahead of schedule. *Travels into Several Remote Nations of the World* confines itself, like a laboratory report, to the chronicle of phenomena noted and sensations undergone.

"I lay down on the grass, which was very short and soft,

[1] Dire à son nom: "Eurêka."

SAMUEL BECKETT: *Comedian of the Impasse*

where I slept sounder than ever I remember to have done in my life, and, as I reckoned, above nine hours; for when I awakened, it was just day-light."

He does not omit the state of the grass, nor an estimate of time, nor the evidence for that estimate. Does he now tell us that he found himself bound fast? No, he inventories in turn the sensations which distinguished this waking from any other waking:

> I attempted to rise, but was not able to stir: for, as I happened to lie on my back, I found my arms and legs were strongly fastened on each side to the ground; my hair, which was long and thick, tied down in the same manner. I likewise felt several ligatures across my body, from my arm-pits to my thighs. I could only look upwards; the sun began to grow hot, and the light offended my eyes. . . . In a little time I felt something alive moving on my left leg. . . .

And only after the six-inch creature has come into sight does he describe it; and

> in the mean time I felt at least forty more of the same kind (as I conjectured) following the first.

"As I conjectured" is Swift's concession to the rules of the game he has established; for until the forty or more additional creatures have in their turn come into Gulliver's view, there can be no assurance that they are indeed of the same kind as the first. Gulliver is the most thoroughgoing empiricist in Europe, and if he fails to realize that his "remote nations of the world" are not at all remote, that his giants and pygmies are simply Europeans altered in scale by, as it were, telescope and microscope, that is because the empiricist can have no means of knowing *what* anything is. The Brobdingnagians, by the same token, conclude that Gulliver himself is a "*relplum scalcath,* which is interpreted literally, *lusus naturae,"* thus conferring a learned name upon their ignorance; while the Lilliputians describe to their sovereign "a hollow pillar of iron, about the length of a man, fastened to a strong piece of timber, larger than the pillar; and upon one side of the pillar were huge pieces of iron sticking out, cut into strange figures"; by which we divine them to intend one of Gulliver's pistols.

So, under the sign of epistemological satire, fiction enters for the first time upon the solemn game of touching and outlining and (where possible) naming *things;* and it conforms, at the expense of some periphrasis, to a set of rules for dealing with the experience of an observer set in the midst of sensory clutter. These rules in turn will soon generate the detective story, which from Wilkie Collins to John Dickson Carr has created its mystery by separating the process of understanding into two parts, describing phenomena first and interpreting them later. And though Beckett more than two centuries after Swift strips down to a bare minimum the inventory of things, he observes with scrupulous care the empiricist definition of a work of fiction, that it is made out of a set of phenomena along with rules for dealing with them. These rules are derived from the mental processes of an observer who is part of the fiction.

Thus The Unnamable, alone in the beginning ("Alone. That is soon said."), ponders "the correct attitude to adopt towards things. And to begin with, are they necessary? What a question. But I have few illusions, things are to be expected. The best is not to decide anything, in this connexion, in advance. If a thing turns up, for one reason or another, take it into consideration." A page later he is wondering whether a certain apparition is perhaps Molloy, wearing Malone's hat. "But it is more reasonable to sup-

SAMUEL BECKETT: *Comedian of the Impasse*

pose it is Malone, wearing his own hat. Oh look, there is the first thing, Malone's hat." And many pages later, having outlined a heart-rending story, he finds himself noting that in addition to four people's emotions it entails "trains, the nature of trains, and the meaning of your back to the engine, and guards, stations, platforms, wars, love, heart-rending cries, that must be the mother-in-law, her cries rend the heart as she takes down her son, or her son-in-law, I don't know, it must be her son, since she cries, and the door, the house-door is bolted, when she got back from the station she found the house-door bolted, who bolted it, he the better to hang himself, or the mother-in-law the better to take him down, or to prevent her daughter-in-law from re-entering the premises, there's a story for you."

There indeed is a story for you, encompassing Verisimilitude and Rationality, and entoiled therefore in alarming lists of objects, all spun out of the mind of The Unnamable as their necessity is perceived. And it is not at all eccentric of Beckett to arrange, in *Comment C'est,* that things shall multiply, and to fearsome totals, as a direct consequence of the fact that the narrator's mind is fanatically orderly. He is simply raising to a more general plane the principle which introduced so many things into *Ulysses;* there are so many things in *Ulysses* because Joyce, in obedience to the rules of the game he was playing, had continual need for more and more of them: hats, pegs, trousers, keys, doors, doorsteps, streets, steeples, sidewalks, loose cellar-flaps, tramcars, cats.

IV

Indeed Beckett has been the first writer to exploit directly the most general truth about the operations of a Stoic

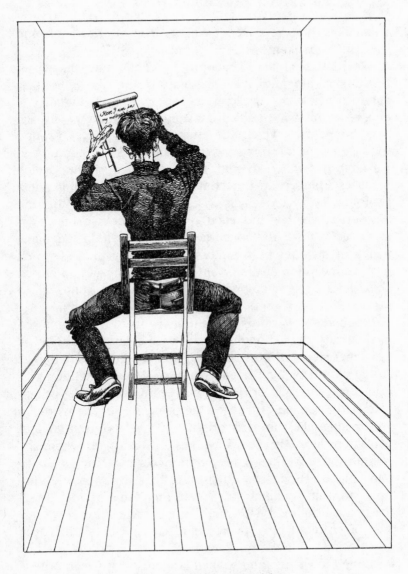

Fig. 8 *Beckett writing*

SAMUEL BECKETT: *Comedian of the Impasse*

Comedian, that he selects elements from a closed set, and then arranges them inside a closed field.

We have seen how lexicography encourages the writer to think of language itself in this way, and how Flaubert came to think of character in this way, and human discourse in this way, guided constantly by analogy with the firm boundaries which the Encyclopaedia places around fluid experience, leaping thought, random knowledge. And we have not failed to note the essential absurdity which menaces Flaubertian procedures, an absurdity, later much exploited by Joyce, which arises from the fact that printed discourse, whether modelled on oral discourse or no, is assembled out of the constituents of the written language, which in turn has been analyzed, by a long process which took its inception at the invention of printing, into a closed field, and discrete counters to be arranged according to rules.

Flaubert's governing convention is absurd, is immersed in absurdity. For though it obeys with clear-sighted fidelity the inherent laws of written discourse, laws which have struggled out of long latency into explicit formulation, yet it affronts, satirizes, criticizes, frequently insults, the principles of the spoken language: the principles of the world in which language takes its origin and has its essential and continuing use: the world, we are apt to forget, where the written language has a very minor, certainly not a dominant, place. Here is the fulcrum of that strain between fiction and what is called "life," even the verbal part of "life," the strain examined with increasing enterprise by a succession of writers from Flaubert and Lewis Carroll to Joyce and Beckett. Flaubert, we remember, is especially fond of bringing the written and spoken languages into each other's presence, when his characters are talking; and what he then exploits of the written language is precisely its air of being synthesized out of little pieces. Books, it seems, can do nothing to human behavior except contaminate it, and contaminate it with cliche. A cliche is simply an element from a closed field. When Emma Bovary says that there is nothing so admirable as sunsets, but especially by the side of the sea, she is not feeling but manipulating the counters of a synthetic feeling, drawn from reading. And Flaubert, we know, carried these principles yet further; made lists of cliches and alphabetized them: defining, so, the closed field of popular discourse, the pieces of which are phrases as the writer's pieces are single words. And we have encountered his closed field of character, three types of romantic adulterer, for example, two types of Frenchman; or his closed field of event, a very small field indeed. Everything, throughout his novels, is menaced by the debacle of the absolutely typical; *Bouvard et Pécuchet* does but repeat the same small cyclic motion, study, enthusiasm, practice, disaster, over and over, until it has used up all the things the curriculum affords us to study: a closed field of plot consuming a closed field of material, as the author pursues a very rigorous game indeed.

Here we may profit by the observations of Miss Elizabeth Sewell on the world of Lewis Carroll, whose works are structured with card games and chess games. Her book on this subject is suggestively titled *The Field of Nonsense,* and before the exposition has gone very far she is talking of "the tight and perfect little systems of Nonsense Verse pure and simple." On the same page with this phrase (21) she invokes *la poésie pure* and the name of Mallarmé. Carroll, she suggests, is "the English manifestation of that French logic and rigor which produced the work of Mallarmé, also labeled nonsense in its time. Carroll is perhaps

SAMUEL BECKETT: *Comedian of the Impasse*

the equivalent of that attempt to render language a closed and consistent system on its own; but he made his experiment not upon Poetry but upon Nonsense."

Whenever we turn we appear to encounter closed and consistent systems. We are clearly in the presence of a dominant analogy, proper to the world of IBM, of probability theory, of concern with modes of short-range and long-range causality, historical, sociological, psychological. It is a world to which none of us needs to be introduced; we live in it rather comfortably, handling punched cards and buying insurance policies. Inside this analogy the Stoic Comedians elected to imprison themselves, the better, in working out its elaborate games, to mime the elaborate world. It requires no more than a closed set of elements and a set of rules for dealing with them, as in chess, acrostics, actuarial tables, Westerns, thrillers, dictionaries and *Finnegans Wake*. We use it to lend structure and direction to our thoughts, as the Victorians used biology and as the men of the Enlightenment used Newtonian physics. The modes of this analogy are everywhere. Its terms are drawn from the mathematical processes that have been working behind the scenes of the modern world in every decade since Pascal undertook to investigate the arithmetic of games of chance. The stronghold on whose battlements it paces, muttering to itself the most abstract formulations of which it is capable, is General Number Theory.

It is from the terminology of Number Theory that the word "field" seems to have found its way into such discussions as these. A field, says the mathematician, contains a collection of elements, and a system of laws for dealing with those elements. Once we have such a theory we can invent as many mathematical systems as we like, and so long as their elements are delimited and their laws internally consistent, their degree of correspondence with the familiar world, where space has three dimensions and every calculation can be verified by counting, is irrelevant. This line of reasoning sets mathematics free from our inescapable structure of intuitions about that familiar world. In the same way, once we shift the postulates of the novel a little, we can have a book like *Ulysses;* but as long as we adhere to the commonsense view that a novel tells a story, *Ulysses* is simply impossible. It is commonplace, however, that the queer things mathematicians do with this freedom have a way of turning back toward the familiar world, and describing it from a new angle. The most famous example is the geometry invented by Lobatchevsky, which used four of Euclid's five postulates but modifies the one about parallel lines; it hung around, an intellectual curiosity, until its practical use was discerned by Einstein. *Ulysses,* similarly, was at first widely mistaken for an unreadable lunacy; forty years have slowly rendered its Dublin's congruence with our London and Los Angeles self-evident.

The Impasse of Beckett's comedy is a closed field by specification. From the moment when we encounter Murphy upside down, naked beneath the rocking chair to which he is bound, crucified, in fact, on a piece of Victorian furniture, to the long blazing interval during which Winnie, buried first to the waist and then to the neck, discourses of Happy Days, Beckett's wry adaptations of Christian iconography have immobilized the body of the sage the better to set his mind free, or relatively free, in a freedom guided by limit, number and system. Molloy is in bed; Malone is in bed; The Unnamable sits forever "like a great horned owl in an aviary"; Hamm is in his chair; Didi and Gogo linger near the tree which Godot apparently specified; Watt's colloquies with Sam, on which all our precious knowledge of the household of Mr. Knott can be shown to depend, took place in what was perhaps a mad-house. And fixed to his spot, each of these persons fondles the elements of a closed field, or scrutinizes the laws for dealing with them.

Thus Watt, given a brief vocabulary of English monosyllables, first commences to invert the order of the words in the sentence, and later the order of the letters in the word, and later that of the sentences in the period; and then he performs simultaneously each possible pair of inversions of this set of three, and finally he combines all three inversions: thus subjecting his little store of monosyllables to every, literally every, possible process of inversion. Or again, the text of *Watt* specifies a certain Kate, "aged twenty-one years, a fine girl but a bleeder," and then silences objection with a footnote: "Haemophilia is, like enlargement of the prostate, an exclusively male disorder. But not in this work." *Comment C'est,* with its three equal parts, Before Pim, With Pim, After Pim, revolves perpetually the same stock of locutions, like the notes in the scale, or like the parts in a watchmaker's cabinet. And *Happy Days,* Beckett's most thoroughgoing exercise in Closed Field logistics, works wholly with quotations and self-quotation. Everything Winnie says she says again, every topic on which she touches she reverts to, at closely calculated intervals. Her first line is a cliche: "Another heavenly day." Her second is a quotation: "For Jesus Christ sake Amen." Her third is another quotation: "World without end Amen." Her fourth is "Begin, Winnie," and her fifth quotes her fourth: "Begin your day, Winnie." Beckett is as deliberate as Bach. Quotation—"what are those wonderful lines?"— is an explicit motif of the play. Winnie speaks of "happiness enow" (Omar Khayyam), calls a scene "to the eye of the mind" (W. B. Yeats), alludes in applying her lipstick to

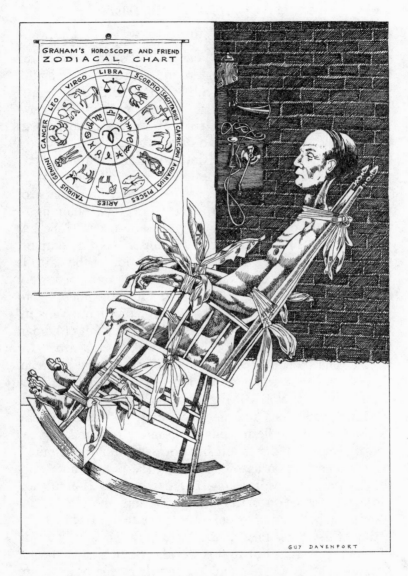

GRAHAM'S HOROSCOPE AND FRIEND
ZODIACAL CHART

GUY DAVENPORT

Fig. 9   Murphy rocking: prior to inversion

SAMUEL BECKETT: *Comedian of the Impasse*

Juliet's "ensign crimson" and "pale flag," cites, beneath the day's blaze, Shakespeare's "Fear no more the heat o' the sun," and when Act II brings round all to do over again, greets the fierce solar ardor with Milton's "Hail, holy light."

Hers is the ultimate impasse. Having rotated its several elements at varying speeds, so that some pass before us twice, some three or four or a dozen times, the play closes in a long tableau of mutual interrogation: Winnie's head alone protruding from the sand, Willie on all fours gazing into her eyes, and thinking perhaps of her, or perhaps of the revolver beside her, and if the latter, then planning to use it perhaps on her (out of pity, or else because she has threatened to sing) or perhaps on himself (out of despair, or weariness with her babble). The rotation of the earth is very slow now, the days very long and very hot, space very empty, memories very remote. To utter the mere word "day" is to "speak in the old style," for the light seems interminable; but some power, interceding on behalf of human metabolism, has furnished a bell for waking and a bell for sleep. The beneficence of this power is questionable, though, since the waking bell clangs imperiously whenever Winnie illicitly closes her eyes. She looks forward, first fondling possessions and then memories, to "the happy day to come when the flesh melts at so many hundred degrees and the night of the moon has so many hundred hours." And it breaks upon us suddenly that the play is not really the lunatic fantasy it seems, but perhaps an H-bomb explosion rendered in extreme slow motion, the blazing instant stretched into an evening's theatre time. Even so, the action of *Endgame* takes place "here in the shelter," outside of which is death. For to this world, as much as to that of *Ulysses* or of Bouvard's and Pécuchet's researches, we are far better habituated than we know. And the sun is stage lighting, and the bell is rung by the prompter; for here as so often the world of art is identical with itself.

Developing with such rigorous passion the themes his Stoic predecessors had themselves first teased into explicitness and then developed with passion at least equal to his, Beckett in seeming to wring dry his art invests it, as did they, with paradoxical fecundity. And raising the book which is a book, the play which is a play, the book as book and the play as play, to new planes of generality, shirking no implication of the fact that all that is written pertains to a mental world, circumscribed in content, constant in method, its boundary the skull, its terms the synapses, and its laws, so far as it can manage, those of logic, he installs us not near Rouen, not in Dublin, but in some more general condition of place and time, a nether landscape, lit by a black moon. Under such a moon, the ghosts walk that were never alive. A child, "never properly born," in an aural world where only voices have status, dies (perhaps) under the wheels of a phantom train. A woman who may be a hallucination exchanges reproaches beside a whispering sea (she does not hear it) with a man who seems less real than old men he imagines. We attend to the buttons on the coat of a fictional character created by a fictional character who is himself perhaps an ingredient in a fiction of his own devising. Godot perpetually does not come, and emissaries who claim to have seen him claim not to have seen the people we can see. A man on a "bed of terror" lulls himself with the vivid chronicle of a journey perhaps never taken, when a solitary cyclist rolled down an eerie street, reading a newspaper in dead of night. Ubiquitous bicycles glisten in the mind, in the reader's mind confronting the writer's mind which confronts a shadow, and proclaim as they disintegrate, wheels sticking, tires leaking, all that the

SAMUEL BECKETT: *Comedian of the Impasse*

intelligence can know of the complaisant and the serene. A man named Sam, in a sort of sanatorium, gropes through the permuted speech of a man named Watt for exact information concerning a man named Knott, who seems never seen. A man with no name describes the spiral Odyssey of a man named Mahood, who may be himself or may have invented him or invented himself or been by him invented. A man with no name, perhaps the same man and perhaps named Sam, tells of life with Pim and of awaiting life with Bom, and while telling this story grows entangled with narrative difficulties, entailing a miraculous multiplication of fishes (tinned), which he exorcises by deciding that his story is a story (like himself). A woman buried to the waist, all of whose speech is quotation or self-quotation, who lives only in her speech and speaks only other's words, nonetheless talks of inviting death: which perhaps can no longer come. Hers "will have been" (she says) Happy Days ("after all") in some future which by definition cannot be.

V

Here the long process we have been tracing comes temporarily to an end. It has been, so far, clearly a process of steady interiorization. We commenced with public documents, encyclopaedias and books of reference, books on every conceivable topic, agriculture, horticulture, mnemonotechnic, literary criticism, a whole library, every bit of it available, and equally available in Rouen and in St. Louis. We moved next in *Ulysses* to a city which 400,000 people inhabit and the rest must take on trust; and we ended with a dark world of sheer speculation. Yet the latter, the most private, is the most accessible of all, supposing as we must

Fig. 10   *The phantom cyclist*

that the laws of reason are universal. We do not even need a library card to enter it.

Or look instead at the human dimension of this series. Flaubert sets on the one hand an encyclopaedia, which being a cacophony of incompatible opinions makes no inner sense whatever in itself, but on the other hand two friends, talking, reading, behaving more or less rationally. Then Joyce partially dissolves the encyclopaedia, which becomes whatever Leopold Bloom can remember: thirty-two feet per second per second, or roy g biv, or Hamlet I am thy father's spirit, or a fragment of *Don Giovanni;* and being part of Leopold Bloom it is not left in its book but assimilated to speech. But silent speech; the interior monologue passes unheard. *Ulysses,* like *Bouvard and Pécuchet,* contains two principal male figures, but they are two strangers. Their trajectories intersect, and they share an hour of good will, and each one then presumably goes his way. Beckett carries both processes further. The dissolution of the encyclopaedia is nearly complete; a few oddments of fact survive, like the umlaut on Würzburg, or the fact that Java is on the Indian Ocean, not the Pacific; but mainly we confront sequences of thought as removed from the particular as possible. A simple experience, a fall from one's crutches, or desire to suck on a stone, is sufficient to generate many hundreds of words. And there are neither two friends here, nor two strangers, but one solitary who at some point in each novel has anomalous dealings with another. Moran goes to Molloy's rescue, and does not find him; a stranger comes and stands for eight hours at the foot of Malone's bed; The Unnamable reports what he claims has been instilled into him by Mahood; the protagonist of *Comment C'est* holds prolonged wordless communion with a certain Pim who may not exist.

Or examine the sequence yet one other way. Moving

from narrative through interior monologue to exacerbated meditation in the dark, it employs with greater and greater generalizing power the technique of inventory. Flaubert's drafts for *Bouvard and Pécuchet* occupied 11,000 pages, most of them notes on reading which he sampled, paraphrased, and distilled; there is no question of completeness here: the idiocies he collected were by hypothesis a few bucketsful from an infinite ocean. But Joyce tends to fondle data which comes in finite sets, and to enumerate these sets, and when the data is as protean as the life of a great city, he avails himself of various delimiting devices—a single day, a city directory, a newspaper—to give at least the appearance of a finite set, over which the book has total control. Beckett, however, need be at no such shifts; he is careful to venture only into situations which exist at such a level of simplicity that one can indeed say of them all that can be said, and rehearse not only what happened but the various combinations of things that might have happened, exhaustively. He would seem to have brought everything within the compass of the book at last; but it is Beckett—and here is the *peripeteia*—it is Beckett whose characters are assailed by proliferation and menaced by mystery. At the very moment when the novel seems to have acquired a strategy for getting everything under its absolute control, at that moment the world dilates and escapes.

This seems to be the theme on which to dwell. The history that culminates in Flaubert is a history of increasing rigor, increasing control. Flaubert is the novelist who knows very well why he has included every scrap of what he has included, and every syllable. He terminates the evolution of the house of fiction from improvised shelters to enduring brick, set upon foundations of reinforced concrete, each stress and strain calculated. He is the patron saint of the rigid fictional machine; and it would seem, a dead end. For after Flaubert a hundred other Flaubertian novels would differ from one another only in locale, theme, and dialogue. The species is stable.

Joyce chose to raise Flaubert to a higher power, generating a fictional machine of such echoing and reentrant complexity as Flaubert never dreamed of. For he glimpsed the paradoxical possibility of the novel, as it grew more highly mechanized, growing gayer, not with the grim necessitarian futility of Flaubert's irony, but with the comedy of utterly inevitable coincidence, as when the chair moves just as the fat man sits. Joyce's is like the comedy of the silent films, in which the flicker of the medium itself reduces men to comically accelerated machines, contending with other machines—cars, revolving doors, ice cream dispensers—; and we know that however often the film is shown it will always go the same way.

At this point Beckett's comedy of incapacity impinges; indeed a comedy of incapacity would seem to stem from Joyce's achievement by a necessary reflex. And Beckett's comedy, if it can deal with everything it touches because it operates solely with the laws of thought, by the same token can really deal with nothing, because thought is not prior to things, and things escape. It is not for nothing that Beckett has so carefully studied Descartes, who held that our thoughts are anterior to the things we think about. And he has realized, and dramatized for us the realization, that the novel itself is a construction of the laws of thought; it is after all something a man thinks up. So that when it supposes that it has secured absolute control of the things it contains, it is deceived, as much deceived as when Descartes supposed that he had made things necessary by thinking his way up to them. And that is why the dead end of

Beckett is so fecund a beginning. It is fecund even in Beckett's own hands; he has time after time rendered another book on his own premises impossible, and then written another book. It may prove incredibly fecund at the hands of successors we cannot dream of.

Etienne Gilson showed us in *The Unity of Philosophical Experience* that philosophy moves continually through similar phases without ever running out of things to do. So probably does fiction; and our three Stoic Comedians demonstrate with unexpected rigor how the art of the novel can move from crisis to crisis, crises of accomplishment, exhaustive accomplishment, without losing the possibility of continuing an orderly development, and doing something utterly unforeseen tomorrow.